Seeing the War

ALSO BY DAVID P. COLLEY

The Road to Victory

Blood for Dignity

Safely Rest

Decision at Strasbourg

Faces of Victory

Sound Waves

Prospect Park: Olmsted and Vaux's Brooklyn Masterpiece

David P. Colley

Seeing the War

THE STORIES

BEHIND THE FAMOUS

PHOTOGRAPHS

OF WORLD WAR II

ForeEdge

ForeEdge

An imprint of University Press of New England

www.upne.com

© 2015 David P. Colley

All rights reserved

Manufactured in the United States of America

Designed by Mindy Basinger Hill

Typeset in Adobe Caslon Pro

Library of Congress Cataloging-in-Publication Data

Colley, David P.

Seeing the war: the stories behind the famous photographs
of World War II / David P. Colley.

    pages   cm

Includes bibliographical references.

ISBN 978-1-61168-726-2 (pbk.: alk. paper)

1. World War, 1939–1945—Photography.

2. World War, 1939–1945—Biography.

3. World War, 1939–1945—Pictorial works. I. Title.

D810.P4C64 2015

940.540092'273—dc23   2015010874

5   4   3   2   1

TO MARY LIZ,

MY MUSE OF SOME

FIFTY YEARS

Contents

ACKNOWLEDGMENTS | xiii

INTRODUCTION | xv

CHAPTER 1

The Yanks Are Coming | 3

Father Joseph Timothy O'Callahan, Medal of Honor Winner | 7

Lt. Col. Robert Moore and Family: Homecoming, 1943 | 13

Graham W. Jackson, Presidential Music Man | 16

CHAPTER 2

Joseph Holmes in the Bulge | 21

"Bige," a Fighting Quaker | 23

Rescue on the *Saratoga* | 26

Roy Willis Humphrey Struggles for Life | 31

CHAPTER 3

Talking Pike with Ike | 35

Rockwell's *Rosie the Riveter* | 38

"One Never Knows What Tomorrow May Bring" | 40

Faris "Bob" Tuohy: Coffee after the Battle | 45

CHAPTER 4

Future Dodger Hits the Beach | 51

A Chance Encounter in Paris | 52

Memphis Belle | 54

Life and Death of *Wee Willie* | 56

Rose of York | 59

CHAPTER 5

Bill Mauldin and Willie and Joe | 63

Earl Leidner: A Face on a Stamp | 65

On a Wing and a Prayer | 66

Nuts! | 70

Lt. Robert Hite, Doolittle Raider | 73

CHAPTER 6

The Dangers of Carrier Landings | 77

Nursing the Wounded | 78

Kilroy | 81

Dinner in the Snow | 83

Long Life for Youthful Lookout | 84

CHAPTER 7

Dorie Miller, Hero at Pearl Harbor | 89

Maynard "Snuffy" Smith Rises to the Occasion | 90

"I Shall Return" | 94

Tom Lea, War Artist | 95

CHAPTER 8

Patton's Infamous Slap | 103

Future President Plays Hoops | 104

First Man across the Rhine | 106

Hans-Georg Henke — May 1945 | 109

He Spotted Nazi Saboteurs | 112

Joseph Demler, Human Skeleton | 115

CHAPTER 9

Sudden Death in Poland—1939 | 121

Casualty of War | 123

Through Death Valley | 127

Patsy Caliendo: The Long Journey Home | 129

CHAPTER 10

Retrieving *Chow-hound* | 137

Three Who Might Have Become Supreme
    Commander instead of Ike | 139

Tony Hillerman, Future Mystery Writer | 142

The Man Who Dropped the Bomb | 145

The Saga of *Lady Be Good* | 149

Lone Survivor at Midway | 151

Bomb Blast on the *Enterprise* | 153

NOTES | 157

ILLUSTRATION CREDITS | 165

Acknowledgments

I began this work about twenty years ago, more as a hobby than any plan to turn it into a book of photographs from World War II, with the goal of determining what became of the men, women, and machines in the images after the war, if they did survive. There are many people whom I spoke to briefly who are not mentioned here but who helped me in my search for veterans and their families. They may have answered the phone, given me tips, or offered tidbits of information. There were scores of them, and I did not record their names.

There are others, however, who offered significant help. One who comes immediately to mind is Faris "Bob" Tuohy, now ninety, who told me about his experiences as a Marine in the Pacific and later in China after the war and who penned the small poem that I include in the book. Other veterans include Kenneth Averill, who spoke on the liberation of Paris, and Julio "Julie" Bescos on carrier duty in the Pacific and the rescue of Kenny Bratton. Wayne Terwilliger recalled the landings on Saipan and later fighting on Okinawa, and Arthur Herz on photographing the Battle of the Bulge. Bob Blanchard told me about his near-death experience on the carrier USS *Franklin* after Japanese aircraft bombed it fifty miles from Japan in February 1945. Evangeline Coeyman related her experiences as an army nurse as her surgical unit followed the fighting in France and Germany in 1944 and 1945.

Many relatives of the men and women in the photographs filled me in about the lives of their husbands, fathers, and brothers who appeared in the images here. Ann Palmer told me about the life of her father, Joseph Holmes. Louise Bratton spoke of her husband "Kenny" Bratton and Lenny Ditano and Robert Faro of Thomas "Red" O'Brien. Danny Sellars reminisced about his father, Milford Abijha "Bige" Sellars, the reluctant Quaker who went to war, as did Wanda Potts, historian at the Mooresville, Indiana, library, in the town where Sellars lived. Lee Weiser told me about Roy Willis Humphrey, his brother-in-law. Storyteller Jay O'Callahan introduced me to his uncle, Father Joseph Timothy O'Callahan, Medal of Honor recipient for his extraordinary bravery and compassion on the burning USS *Franklin*. Nancy Lee Franks Goodall spent many hours with me relating the life of her brother Lt. Jesse "Red" Franks from Columbus, Mississippi. Anne Hillerman gave me information and photographs of her father, mystery writer Tony Hillerman. Kate and Justin Lawson and Brenda Cranford sent me photographs of Lawrence Britton, the boy sailor, whom I interviewed about his war experiences.

Attorney John Dennis in Albany, New York, gave me valuable information about George Lott, the wounded army medic who was the subject of two major *Life* magazine articles and who virtually disappeared after the war. Attorney Michael Gross of the Author's Guild provided needed advice about copyright. Timothy Kenny of the Paul E. Ison Marine Corps League Detachment 60 provided information and photos of this famous Marine.

Others who assisted, together with their organization or employer: Nathan Dwelle, of the Fort Worth Cats; Julia Pine, the Southern California Golf Association; Bridget Cass, the College of Holy Cross; Dagmar L. Greenaway, *Virgin Island Daily News;* Barbara Ann "Sparky" Scattene and Bill Fisk Sr. and Bill Fisk Jr. at Fisk's Camera Shop, Easton, Pennsylvania; Jonathan Gordon, Alston & Bird LLP; Sondra Zaharias, Getty Images; Matt Lutts, AP Images; Rosemary Morrow, Redux Pictures; Karyn Reolke, Stars and Stripes Honor Flights; Caroline Waddell, U.S. Holocaust Memorial Museum; Kathy Sechowski and Santiago Flores, *South Bend Tribune;* Arturo Flores, of the Tom Lea Institute; Keith Hunsaker, of Kemp & Associates; Patricia Dugdale, Army Deceased Files; Nora Chidlow, U.S. Coast Guard Historian's Office; William Shaw, publisher, *Mercer Island Reporter;* Claude Zachary, USC Library; Theresa Roy and Holly Reed, Still Pictures Reference Team, National Archives; Cyndy Gilley, Do You Graphics; Dorothy Sliney and James C. Marshall, Toledo-Lucas Public Library; and Clifford Jackson. An author always needs his libraries, and I owe thanks to the libraries of Lafayette College, Lehigh University, and the city of Easton, Pennsylvania.

Special thanks to my agent Richard Curtis of Richard Curtis Associates, New York, who has successfully guided me and my work for decades, and to my wife, Elizabeth Keegin Colley, whose support is always there. Also, many thanks to Stephen Hull, my editor at University Press of New England, for his careful assistance and encouragement.

Introduction

We've seen their faces for three-quarters of a century — the men and women in the photographs from World War II. They are frozen in time, in a chow line during the Battle of the Bulge, marching down the Champs-Élysées the day after the liberation of Paris in August 1944, wincing in pain as they are pulled from a stricken torpedo bomber, or exhausted, grimy, and sipping coffee after a bloody Pacific island battle.

These are the veterans of the Greatest Generation, seen when they were hardly more than boys and girls. Most have now passed from this earth. The remaining few will soon follow, and their lives and experiences will be as distant to us as those soldiers 150 years ago who peer out from cracked and smudged Civil War daguerreotypes. As a child during the war, I watched newsreels of sinking ships and flaming airplanes, terrified civilians fleeing bombardment, and scenes of mortal aerial and ground combat. I recall air raid drills at home with sirens wailing in the night like baying wolves. After the war the men came home, my father's generation, when they were young, many barely out of their teens. They were our heroes, and many had endured horrors absolutely unimaginable to current generations.

World War II is endlessly fascinating in its scope, its impact on the men who fought it, and on America. Many of these warriors served in places seemingly as far from home then as the moon is to us today. World War II shrank the globe, and America would never be the same. Mixed with the ugliness and horror of war was a certain romance of faraway places like Kolombangara, Vella Lavella, Sulu, Surigau, Bizerte, and Casablanca. Never before had such huge armies and vast fleets of ships and aircraft gone forth to engage the enemy. The world will never again see such a massive endeavor.

As the men aged, I became interested in their stories, wrote books and articles about their experiences, collected histories, and pored over the thousands of photographs. Vicariously, I got to know many of the men in the photos, at least their faces, and often wondered what became of them, and some of their machines, after the camera shutter snapped. Did they live to experience the joys and simple pleasures of life after such a devastating experience? Or did they never have the opportunity?

One of my books was about a young flier, Lt. Jesse D. Franks, who left his Baptist seminary to enlist in the Army Air Forces in 1942. His full-page portrait appears in the *American Heritage Picture History of World War II*. While in the army during the Vietnam War, I was intrigued by Franks's portrait but also curious. Nice young American boys like Franks are supposed to go forth and vanquish the enemy and return home in triumph to live out their lives. Did Jesse Franks?

The famous photograph of the full Twenty-Eighth Division marching down the Champs-Élysées, the day after the liberation of Paris, which later became the basis of a commemorative stamp issued in 1945, shows seemingly endless ranks of brown-clad American infantrymen against the backdrop of the Arc de Triomphe. But the parade was something of a forced march. The route through Paris was the fastest way to the front, and that evening these same infantrymen were in combat. What were their stories? How many were wounded, killed, or survived unscathed?

It became my hobby and a passion to discover the fate of the men in many World War II photographs, some iconic, some not so. In a few cases it was easy to locate the men; in many cases it was not. The well-publicized photograph of an exhausted Yank soldier leaning against a building in Belgium during the Battle of the Bulge should have been easy. I live in Pennsylvania, and the man was an infantryman in the Twenty-Eighth Division of the Pennsylvania National Guard. But division historians themselves had tried to discover his identity, without success. After several years of searching I came across a dog-eared book in the Lehigh University library that printed his photograph and gave his name and hometown—Mooresville, Indiana, just south of Indianapolis. The Indiana phone book listed many with the same name. I started telephoning and, from random calls, finally reached his son in Indianapolis, who told me his father's story.

The toughest find was George Lott, an army medic wounded in the autumn of 1944 in France. *Life* magazine followed Lott from a front-line aid station through surgeries in Paris, in Great Britain, and in the United States. He appeared on the cover of *Life* on January 29, 1945, with a lengthy story, supplemented by numerous photographs, about his recovery from shell fire. The magazine did a follow-up story in 1947, when Lott was still in a military hospital. After that he disappeared. Others, including myself, wanted to know what happened to him.

I contacted the Veterans Administration, without success, called hospitals in New York State and in Michigan, where Lott had convalesced, and checked the Social Security death index. A census report from the late 1930s showed that he had lived as a boy in Binghamton, New York, and had been a foster child. I called various Lott families in New York, but the man had vanished into the mists. Then one day I discovered the website of a law firm in Utah that had done work for Lott. From information it provided I pieced together an outline of George Lott's reclusive life.

The pursuit of the soldiers in World War II photographs is illuminating. We never stop and ask about the toll of war or what happened to the men in the photographs. Many were killed or wounded, or they suffered deep psychological wounds that they carried till the day they died. The year 2015 represents the seventieth anniversary of the end of World War II. Undoubtedly, it will be the last significant time that this nation honors its surviving World War II veterans. Soon they will be no more, and the war will be mostly forgotten. It already is ancient history to most Americans. But the veterans of World War II, depicted in photographs, bring alive those momentous years and enshrine the soldiers in our history and in our imaginations.

Seeing the War

Chapter 1

The Yanks Are Coming

What a parade! It was eerily reminiscent of a similar procession of triumphant German troops marching down the Champs-Élysées four years before as the occupation of France and Paris began. But in this new parade, on August 29, 1944, tens of thousands of American troops marched down the same grand Parisian boulevard four days after the Allies liberated Paris. French general Jacques LeClerc and his Second Free French Armored Division were first in Paris on August 25, having raced to the capital against First U.S. Army orders. The French capital was in a frenzy of celebration after the Nazi tyranny was driven out and as the Germans retreated across France with American and British forces close on their heels. This photograph of members of the 112th and 110th Regiments, Twenty-Eighth Infantry Division, in combat regalia, marching twenty-four abreast, is arguably one of the most famous of World War II, taken by Peter J. Carroll of the Associated Press. What was seemingly a victory parade was in fact a strategic necessity to confront the Germans just outside Paris. The fastest route to the front was straight through the city and down the Champs-Élysées.[1]

The photograph was immortalized in a commemorative stamp as a symbol of American might and of the United States as the beacon of freedom in the world. These troops came to foreign shores to rid the world of the Nazi menace. The Post Office Department issued similar stamps for all the military services, and this shot was designed for a stamp honoring the U.S. Army in World War II.

In the mind's eye, these soldiers marched on to defeat the Germans and then returned home to family and friends, to resume their lives and eventually die as old men. But this was not to be so for some. Several in the front ranks were killed, and many others were wounded in the subsequent fighting to liberate Europe.

Just after the stamp was issued on September 28, 1945, researchers and buffs set out to identify as many of the soldiers in the photograph as possible. The search went on for years and still goes on, although the passing of time makes it unlikely that more men will be discovered. Some twenty-seven men have been identified.

The men on the right are from the Twenty-Eighth Division's 112th Regiment; the men on the left are from the 110th Regiment. Behind them is the division's 109th Regiment. Not only did they march on that same day to fight the Germans on the outskirts of Paris; they were engaged a few weeks later in some of the most savage and costly fighting of the war. The division was badly mauled in the Battle of the Heurtgen Forest in the fall of 1944, and again in the Battle of the Bulge in December 1944. Among the men in the Twenty-Eighth Division, but not in the parade, was Pvt. Eddie Slovak, the only U.S. soldier executed for desertion during World War II.[2]

The stories of a few who were identified exemplify the strength and endurance of the men who fought World War II.

The first man was identified on September 28, 1945.[3] Three wounded veterans in Walter Reed Army Hospital in Washington were invited to attend first-day-of-issue ceremonies at the Pentagon. When they returned to the hospital they met a resident internist who asked to see a copy of the stamp. The internist was Dr. Paschal A. Linguiti, of Philadelphia, who suddenly saw himself center left in the photograph wearing the Red Cross armbands. Dr. Linguiti (no. 1) was in the 112th Regiment's medical corps.

In the ensuring months other soldiers in the first row were identified, including two who were later killed in action. Capt. Howard E. Ludwick (2), in front on the far right, was killed in Creil, France, on August 31, two days after this photo was taken. Ludwick, twenty-seven years old, from Washington Court House, Ohio, was a dance instructor before the war and had been in the army since 1941. He is buried in the Normandy American Cemetery at Colleville-sur-Mer, France.

Lt. Ralph W. Spaans (3), just to the left of Dr. Linguiti, was killed on November 2, 1944, in the Heurtgen Forest in Germany. Spaans, twenty-three, was born in Medford, Massachusetts, but was raised in Bogota, New Jersey. His body was recovered in the Heurtgen Forest by Graves Registration teams in 1945, four months after he was killed. He is buried in Henri-Chapelle U.S. Military Cemetery in Belgium.

A few others: Lt. James Ruby, in the center (4), front and looking to his right, was commanding officer of C Company, 112th Regiment. He was twice wounded in action in Germany by mortar shells. Ruby was born in Seymour,

Iowa, in 1920 and graduated from the University of Iowa, where he was Phi Beta Kappa and captain of the varsity rifle team that won the Big Ten and Western Conference championships. After being wounded, Ruby was returned to the United States, where he was hospitalized for several months and released from duty in September 1945.

In the second row, by number:

5. Lt. James C. Sharpe, of Kissimmee, Florida, was wounded near Bollendorf, Germany, in September 1944. After being hospitalized he returned to Company L, 112th Regiment, which was engaged shortly thereafter in the Battle of the Bulge. He served with the Twenty-Eighth through the remainder of the war and returned to the States and was discharged in late 1945.

6. Lt. George W. Thoemke, twenty-two, from Lake Mills, Iowa, was commissioned a second lieutenant in July 1943 and joined the Twenty-Eighth Division in August 1944. After the march through Paris, Thoemke said that "we averaged about fifteen miles a day into Belgium and entered Germany at Bollendorf."[4] On September 17 he was wounded in a German counterattack. After recuperating, he was assigned to limited duty on the Red Ball Highway and arrived back in the States in December 1945.

7. Sgt. Peter Friscan, thirty-four, from Detroit, was a barber in civilian life. During the Battle of the Bulge, Friscan was wounded and taken prisoner. He was liberated by the Russians on April 18, 1945, and was discharged from the army in November 1945.

8. Sgt. Charley Jordon, twenty-five, was a welder before the war. He joined the Twenty-Eighth just after Saint-Lô and served with C Company through the fighting in France, Belgium, and Luxembourg. He was captured in September 1944 at Bollendorf, shipped to Stalag 3C east of Berlin, and liberated by the Russians on January 31, 1945. He returned to the United States on April 9, 1945.

9. Lt. Walter E. Tobler, thirty-one, commanded an 81mm mortar section in Company D, 112th Infantry. He sustained slight wounds on two occasions before being assigned to C Company under the command of Lieutenant Ruby. Tobler survived the rest of the war unscathed.

10. Tech. Sgt. Edward F. Schroeder, thirty-four, was wounded in the Heurtgen Forest. He recalled that the morning of the parade through Paris, the troops shaved and formed up at 10 a.m. "I remember the march well, the French people lined the streets, yelling Vive Amérique and dishing out the champagne by the bottle. That night we dug in at what was left of the Le Bourget Airfield. The next day we were again proceeding toward Germany."[5]

These are but brief summaries of only the war years of these men. The following stories will relate, when possible, the lives of the men and women after the war.

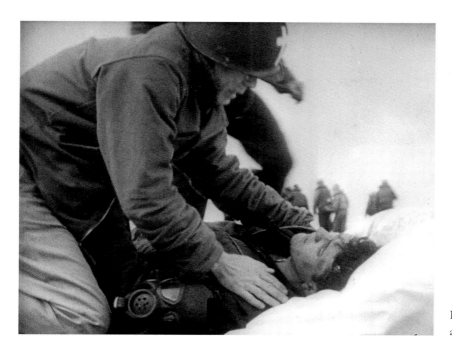

Father O'Callahan
and Bob Blanchard.

Father Joseph Timothy O'Callahan, Medal of Honor Winner

On March 19, 1945, the aircraft carrier USS *Franklin* was operating with Task Force 58 as part of a massive American fleet launching air strikes against Japan sixty miles from the enemy's home islands. Without warning, a Japanese plane penetrated the fleet's fighter screen and dropped two 500-pound bombs that smashed through the wooden flight deck and exploded in the ship's interior. Instantly, the *Franklin* was engulfed in explosions and fire, and hundreds of men were wounded or killed.

Lt. Cmdr. Joseph Timothy O'Callahan, the ship's chaplain, organized salvage and rescue parties to fight the conflagration that threatened to sink the ship. They fought through withering heat, explosions, and dense smoke before the fires were brought under control. O'Callahan then turned his attention to the scores of wounded and dying men scattered about the flight deck. For many, the only succor O'Callahan could offer was last rites.

Father O'Callahan.

Of the iconic photographs that depict the naval history of World War II in the Pacific theater, none is more poignant than that of Father O'Callahan administering last rites to a sailor. O'Callahan is silhouetted against the sky with hands clasped, kneeling in prayer over the young man, whose identity was unknown at the time. The dead were buried at sea and the scores of wounded transferred to hospital ships.

The *Franklin* was saved in no small part by O'Callahan's leadership, and for his valor he was awarded the Medal of Honor. The citation for the medal reads as follows:

A valiant and forceful leader, calmly braving the perilous barriers of flame and twisted metal to aid his men and his ship, Lieutenant Commander O'Callahan groped his way through smoke-filled corridors to the open flight deck and into the midst of violently exploding bombs, shells, rockets and other armament. With the ship rocked by incessant explosions, with debris and fragments raining down and fires raging in ever increasing fury, he organized and led firefighting crews into the blazing inferno on the flight deck; he directed the jettisoning of live ammunition and the flooding of the magazine; he manned a hose to cool hot, armed bombs rolling dangerously on the listing deck, continuing his efforts, despite searing, suffocating smoke which forced men to fall back gasping and imperiled others who replaced them. Serving with courage, fortitude, and deep spiritual strength, Lieutenant Commander O'Callahan inspired the gallant officers and men of the Franklin to fight heroically and with profound faith in the face of almost certain death and to return their stricken ship to port. The Franklin's skipper described Father Joe as "the bravest man I have ever seen."[6]

O'Callahan's exploits and courage on the *Franklin* served as the basis for numerous national magazine articles and a movie, *Battle Stations,* which was released in 1956. Another film, *The Saga of the Franklin,* an official navy film, shows O'Callahan performing Herculean tasks while under fire. O'Callahan

also penned his own book, *I Was Chaplain on the Franklin,* published in 1956.[7]

USS *Franklin* burning off the coast of Japan.

Known to his shipmates as "Father Joe," O'Callahan was forty-one when the *Franklin* was bombed. A native of Boston, he graduated from Boston College High School and studied for the priesthood, eventually teaching at the College of Holy Cross in Worcester, Massachusetts. He became head of the mathematics department there, but with the outbreak of World War II in Europe he entered the navy as a chaplain in 1940, the year before Pearl Harbor.

During the war he served as chaplain aboard the aircraft carrier *Ranger* and took part in the North African campaign before becoming chaplain on the *Franklin*. He left the navy in 1946 with the rank of captain. He was the first navy chaplain to be awarded the Medal of Honor.

Father O'Callahan received severe injuries on the *Franklin*. The heat and smoke permanently damaged his lungs, which led to serious breathing problems for the rest of his life. Shortly after returning to Holy Cross in 1946, he suffered a disabling stroke. He retired from teaching in 1950, at the age of forty-six, and became, as he put it, "dead in the water," like his old ship, the *Franklin*. He died of another stroke on March 18, 1964.

Father O'Callahan will not be forgotten. The science library in Haberlin Hall at Holy Cross was named in his honor, and Jay O'Callahan, his nephew, a professional storyteller who remembers his uncle particularly from his undergraduate days at Holy Cross, performs the story "Father Joe: A Hero's Journey" to national and international audiences.[8] There is a happier addendum to this story. The sailor O'Callahan was praying over in the photo survived. Yeoman second class Bob Blanchard was among several hundred men trapped deep beneath the flight deck and never expected to

Bob Blanchard
in 2006.

live as explosions rocked the ship and smoke clogged the air. Rescue teams fought their way below and broke through to Blanchard and his comrades. Blanchard was so overcome that when he reached the open air he collapsed on the flight deck near where Father O'Callahan was administering last rites to sailors. Without realizing that Blanchard was not among the dying, O'Callahan administered to him and then moved on to others. Blanchard lived out his life in New Jersey and died, at the age of ninety, in 2014.[9]

A navy destroyer escort was named in Father Joe's honor. The USS *O'Callahan* (DE-1051) was the first United States ship to be christened by a nun, Father Joe's sister, Sister Rose Marie. The final ship of the Garcia class of ocean escorts, the *O'Callahan* was commissioned in 1968 at the Boston Naval Shipyard and served several tours in the Pacific, including duty off Vietnam.

USS *O'Callahan.*

Lt. Col. Robert Moore and Family: Homecoming, 1943

This Pulitzer Prize–winning image shows Lt. Col. Robert Moore, U.S. Army, embracing his seven-year-old daughter, Nancy, after returning home as a hero from the North African campaign in 1943. Moore hugs Nancy as his wife, Dorothy, and his two-year-old nephew, Michael Bruce Croxdale, wait their turn.[10] *Omaha World-Herald* photographer Earle Bunker took this photo on July 15, 1943, just after Moore stepped off a train in the tiny hamlet of Villisca, Iowa, where in civilian life he operated his family's drugstore.

As *World-Herald* reporter Stephen Buttry later wrote,

> The photograph, one of the most enduring images from World War II, symbolizes the hopes of a generation whose men fought that war. Not a single face shows in the Pulitzer Prize–winning photo, but the joy is overwhelming — a daddy in a round military cap stooping to wrap his arms around a spindly-legged daughter reaching up to his broad shoulders in

The Moore family: Dorothy, Robert, and Nancy.

a welcoming hug. Mom waits her turn, a hand to her face in delight. An excited little boy watches.

At depots across America, the scene was repeated countless times as fathers and sons and husbands returned from battle. Implicit in the joy of each homecoming was the understanding that more than a quarter of a million families grieved for soldiers who would not come home.[11]

Called to duty at the war's beginning, Moore trained at Camp Claiborne, Louisiana, before embarking for Northern Ireland in May 1942, as a captain commanding Company F, a unit in the Thirty-Fourth Infantry Division. In November his unit landed in Algeria as part of the invasion of North Africa, and Moore was awarded the Silver Star for gallantry in the landings. He rallied scattered men and directed a flanking action that destroyed an enemy machine gun nest.

Moore took over command of the Second Battalion, and when U.S. forces entered Tunisia, he and his men advanced from Algeria and were assigned to protect a key mountaintop lookout post at Djebel Lessourda. For two days shells, mortars, and enemy infantry assaults pounded the battalion. They held, but the American troops at the base of the mountain pulled back, leaving Moore and his men stranded. Ordered to withdraw, Moore organized his men, and they infiltrated out of their mountaintop positions and through German lines after dark, walking by unsuspecting enemy troops, who believed the passing soldiers were German. Moore carried his prized bed sack as he led the escape. "I decided to bring it along if it was the last thing I did," he said. In the homecoming picture the bed sack is at Moore's feet as he hugs his daughter.

Moore rose to the rank of lieutenant colonel, and because combat-tested officers were needed at home to train troops, he returned to the States, arriving in Villisca on Burlington Train No. 6.

Moore was assigned to various training commands, and when the war ended he took up where he left off in 1940, running the family drugstore in Villisca. He also remained in the Iowa National Guard, where he eventually became a brigadier general, and retired in 1963.

Much of the attraction of this photograph, and others taken during World

War II, is that time is stopped. We are caught only in that moment of glory and of heroes, and in the case of the Moore family, in a moment of great joy with the safe return of a soldier, husband, father, and uncle. We do not ask, nor do we want to ask at times, what transpired after the photograph was taken. Reality would intrude.

Moore experienced his share of setbacks and tragedies in a long life. As Steve Buttry wrote years later, "Moore knew great sorrow. A returning war hero receives no exemption from life's heartaches—bankruptcy, alcoholism, alienation from the daughter whose embrace was so warm."[12]

The drugstore failed as America changed and the automobile became king and malls sprang up around cities and towns. Moore was forced into bankruptcy and closed the store in 1962. He then went to work as a city clerk in the county seat of Red Oak, fifteen miles northeast of Villisca, and eventually took a job as a bailiff at the Montgomery County Courthouse. Moore battled alcoholism, as did his wife, Dorothy, who suffered a disabling stroke in the late 1960s. She recovered but died of cancer in 1982 at age seventy-one.

Moore's daughter, Nancy, also struggled with illness. She was stricken with multiple sclerosis in the 1970s, and the disease eventually led to her death in 1984. Because she was partially crippled, her car was equipped with hand controls, and she lost control of the vehicle one icy morning. Although she walked away from the crash, she died from internal injuries on December 13, 1984. She was forty-eight. Her relationship with her father was harmed by his heavy drinking.

The little boy in the photograph also faced serious health challenges. Michael Croxdale was a spirited, bright kid who was afflicted by seizures. He later became a doctor and served in Vietnam, where he was awarded the Soldier's Medal for saving the lives of wounded GIs under fire. In Vietnam he was exposed to Agent Orange, which may have contributed, along with a four-pack-a-day smoking habit, to his lung cancer years later. He too dealt with alcoholism. Michael died June 29, 1993, at the age of fifty-two.

Colonel Moore lived into his eighties and was a well-known figure on the Red Oak golf links. He had a stroke and died on April 18, 1991. He was eighty-six years old.

Graham W. Jackson, Presidential Music Man

Graham Washington Jackson Sr. was too old to fight in World War II, but because of his talents he was accepted in the navy as a musician and assigned to recruiting duties.[13] He was also well connected to Franklin Roosevelt, having first met the president in 1933 and regularly entertained him at the Little White House in Warm Springs, Georgia, Roosevelt's retreat. Jackson often took members of the Atlanta First Congregational Church choir to sing for the president.

This well-known and dramatic photograph expresses not only Jackson's grief at losing a good friend but symbolizes the sorrow and disbelief experienced by Americans on learning of the president's death on April 12, 1945.

The photo was taken by *Life* photographer Edward Clark as Jackson sang hymns for the throngs of mourners that had gathered outside the Little White House as the president's body was borne away to the train that would carry it to Washington, D.C., and final burial in Hyde Park, New York, the Roosevelt family's ancestral home. The hymn most remembered that Jackson sang that day was "Going Home," the Negro spiritual immortalized by Czech composer Antonin Dvorak in his *New World* Symphony.

Jackson later recalled, "The photographer stumbled over my foot and looked up. . . . He saw my face and saw those tears coming down my cheeks and just reached around on his shoulder and got one of his cameras up and — blip — and thought no more of it."[14]

Jackson was born in 1903, in Portsmouth, Virginia; his middle name commemorated the fact that he was born on Washington's birthday. He said that he came by music naturally and at an early age because his mother was a choir soloist and he spent much of his time with her in church. He debuted as a piano player at age seven, accompanying silent movies, and by the time he was in high school he was playing professionally at venues such as a Norfolk, Virginia, dancing school.

Jackson moved to Atlanta in 1924 as leader of a musical group, the Seminole Syncopators, that toured with the Liston Jazz Revue. In Atlanta he landed another job as orchestra leader and pit pianist at the city's famed 81 Theater. He also enrolled in Morehouse College to begin what was a long but futile effort to obtain a college degree.

In 1928 he was offered the position of music instructor at Washington High School in Atlanta, where he taught until 1940. All through these years he developed a musical reputation performing on the piano, organ, and accordion in commercial and private clubs and restaurants.

Jackson continued to be an attraction in the Atlanta area long after the war and played for Presidents Harry Truman, Dwight Eisenhower, John Kennedy, Lyndon Johnson, and Jimmy Carter. At the Republican National Convention in 1960 Jackson played the "Star-Spangled Banner," which caused something of a flap. Republicans, noting his long association with President Roosevelt, crowed that the entertainer had defected to the GOP.

Jackson liked political figures, and they liked him. In 1969 Governor

Lester Maddox, despite his image as a segregationist, appointed Jackson to the Georgia Board of Corrections. President Carter later named Jackson official state musician.

Jackson lived on C Street in Atlanta in a house that he remodeled in 1947 to resemble the Little White House. He later succeeded in having the street renamed White House Drive.

Three years before his death, Jackson suffered a stroke and lost his voice, but he continued to play the piano. He died on January 16, 1983, following another stroke. He was eighty.

Chapter 2

Joseph Holmes in the Bulge

More than nineteen thousand Americans were killed and sixty thousand wounded, missing in action, or taken prisoner during the Battle of the Bulge, which raged from December 16, 1944, to mid-January 1945. The Bulge — named for the German salient in the American front line in Belgium — was Hitler's last attempt to divide and defeat the Western Allies when he launched the attack with a quarter of a million men. The American and British armies had driven the Germans back from Normandy in France to the German frontier with Belgium and Luxembourg and were preparing to drive into the Nazi heartland when Hitler struck. The ensuing struggle took place in some of the severest weather Europe had experienced in years, with snow and ice covering the forested battlefields and overcast skies initially preventing use of Allied air power.

It was in this Armageddon-like struggle that Sgt. Joseph Holmes found himself in December 1944. An infantryman with the Thirty-Fifth Infantry Division, the Cumberland, Maryland, native had been a bartender living comfortably with his wife and his daughter, Ann, just nine months before. He had been in combat for three months when he was photographed January 10, 1945, in the snowbound Ardennes forest.[1]

"This photograph appeared when my father had been out in the cold for thirty-two days," said Ann Palmer, Holmes's daughter. The image became well known when it appeared in one of Stephen Ambrose's books, and the caption noted that the photo depicted a tough, battle-hardened U.S. infantryman.

Holmes entered the army in March 1944 and six months later arrived in France. Within days he was in combat. The Thirty-Fifth, attached to Gen. George Patton's Third Army, was engaged in heavy combat in eastern France before being sent to the Ardennes area to help blunt the new German offensive and relieve the 101st Airborne Division, which had been surrounded at Bastogne, Belgium. Later in the war the Thirty-Fifth moved into Germany, where Holmes was awarded the Silver Star for heroism in combat. The citation for Holmes's Silver Star read as follows:

Sgt. Joseph Holmes in the Battle of the Bulge.

Sergeant Holmes, a member of a mortar platoon, accompanied by another member of the section, voluntarily advanced to within 25 yards of the enemy emplacement and directed such intense fire upon the enemy that the machine gun crew surrendered. A short time later another enemy machine gun opened fire from the same position, and Sergeant Holmes and his companion again moved forward under fire and engaged the enemy crew in a fire fight in the course of which a German officer was wounded, and the enemy machine gun crew surrendered. Sergeant Holmes' gallantry contributed immeasurably to the success of the river crossing and to the occupation of the village of Dieding with minimum casualties.

The war ended, and a "battle-hardened" Holmes returned home to Cumberland, possibly suffering from what today is recognized as PTSD — post-traumatic stress disorder — and picked up where he had left off. Standing above six feet, one inch in height, Holmes was well known as a standout high school basketball and baseball player. He went back to work as a bartender; despite his proximity to alcohol, he was a teetotaler.

Holmes, like so many soldiers, was haunted by his combat experiences, and his daughter is convinced that the war eventually killed him, as surely as a German bullet. "He never talked about the war. He was a very, very tormented man because of it, the horrors they went through. . . . I think he felt bad for what he did, I think the guilt lay so heavy on him he couldn't take it." Whenever he was asked about the action for which he was awarded the Silver Star, Holmes would refer to it as "something I did." Ann remembers her father as "the nicest man you would ever want to meet. He was a kind, wonderful husband and a wonderful father."

In the early 1960s Holmes experienced bouts of paranoia, and in 1966 he had a nervous breakdown and never recovered. He was in and out of hospitals for nine years. "Every-

Joseph Holmes in the 1960s.

thing about his illness was war connected," Ann said. "When he'd have the breakdowns he would talk about seeing silver stars on the floors and ceiling and hear airplanes coming over, and he thought they were coming to get him. He would say crazy things about seeing dead Germans everywhere."

It was during one of Holmes's "spells" in 1975 that he got out of a hospital bed one night and fell to the floor, striking his head. He died two days later at age sixty-one.

Some years later Holmes's photograph appeared, and Ann received a letter from an old war buddy of her father's, Alexander Karavish of Dayton, Ohio, with a photocopy of the photograph. Karavish talked about his days with Holmes and ended by writing: "You had a wonderful dad and he thought a lot about you. I hope you and your son can now enjoy grandpa's picture."

"Bige," a Fighting Quaker

Milford Abijha Sellars, nicknamed "Bige," symbolized the American citizen-soldier in this classic photo taken during the Battle of the Bulge. His rugged, handsome face is that of an infantryman, exhausted after weeks of combat, days without food or sleep, and yearning for home in Indiana.[2]

Under his helmet Bige had black curly hair. His eyes were brown. He was about five feet, eight inches tall. "He had quite a Roman nose," his son, Daniel Sellars, said, "and he had very distinctive ears in his old age."

Bige was a member of the 110th Regiment, Twenty-Eighth Division, which had been assigned to the front in the Ardennes in December 1944. He fought through France, marched in triumph through Paris in August, and went to fight in the costly battles of the Heurtgen Forest. The fighting there had so reduced the division that it was placed in the "quiet" sector of the Ardennes along the German frontier to refit and regroup. It wasn't quiet for long. On December 16, the opening day of the Bulge, found the Twenty-Eighth in the epicenter of the German onslaught. As the division fell back, absorbing the German attacks, the 110th was nearly destroyed. Bige was one of a handful of men from his company to survive.

The photograph was taken as Bige and a comrade were attempting to find their way back to their unit, Daniel Sellars said. They hadn't eaten in several

days and had just tried to bargain with a Belgian baker for several loaves of bread as he rode by on his bicycle. The look of exhaustion on Bige's face was in part due to the frustration of his unsuccessful attempt to barter. Just after the photo was taken, Bige and his companion set out again to find their unit, and as they walked down the street an artillery shell landed in the exact spot where they had been standing in the photograph. Had they not moved on, both men would have been killed.

Born in 1910 in Mooresville, Indiana, whose most notorious citizen during the Depression was the bank robber John Dillinger, Bige was a good baseball player and turned down a chance to play professionally in California. He was married in 1933, a simple man who had been a farmer and carpenter before the war and afterward returned to Mooresville. In 1973 he retired from farming and carpentry and went to work in the maintenance department of the town's Automotive Armature Company.

Bige was a Quaker whose ancestors had settled in Mooresville in the early 1800s from North Carolina. While he was not strong in his religious beliefs, his son said, "He was a Quaker in the back of his heart . . . a very kind man without a mean bone in his body." Bige once received a letter from a former German POW thanking him for his kindness. The German recalled that Bige had given him a cigarette when other American captors were being harsh.

Bige seldom spoke of his combat experience. His son added, "He saw horrible things in the service, and he didn't talk about ugly things. He was very Quaker in this respect," although he once described seeing a fellow infantryman killed when he stepped on a mine. "It blew [the man] to bits. He couldn't tell who or what he had been." Bige always remembered the day the war ended in Europe, May 8, 1945. It was his thirty-fifth birthday.

The war left its mark on Bige. Daniel said that he learned, after his father returned home, never to waken him from a nap. "He was very skittish, and you were liable to get hit when Mother would say 'Go wake your father.' So I'd take a broom or yardstick and poke him."

Bige was little known in Mooresville for the photograph and better remembered for having saved the life of a young girl in a fire later in the war. He broke his leg in the rescue and was shipped to England to convalesce. When Bige died in 1997, his son said, "He just wore out. He was a good man who lived and worked in the same town all his life and died two miles from the place he was born." There was no mention in his obituary in the *Indianapolis Times* that he was the man in the famous photograph.

Bige's first wife died in the late 1950s, and he remarried in a year. He lived his life so close to home that a trip to New York City in 1955 was a major event in the Sellars family. "We stayed at the Plaza Hotel for forty-nine dollars a night," Daniel remembers. "We had a big room, and we all got dressed up every afternoon to have tea in the hotel lobby."

Rescue on the *Saratoga*

By the summer of 1943 the Americans had turned the tide in the war against Japan. Victories at Guadalcanal and Bougainville in the Solomon Islands in the South Pacific led to further American attacks through the Central Pacific. One Japanese bastion that stood in the way of the American advance was the Japanese naval base at Rabaul on the island of New Britain, now a province of Papua, New Guinea. American forces began attacks on Rabaul in the summer and fall of 1943, with the first strike by naval aircraft on November 2 from the aircraft carriers USS *Saratoga* and *Princeton.* In the attack the Avenger torpedo bomber piloted by Cmdr. Howard Caldwell was badly damaged by cannon fire from a Japanese Zero fighter plane. Caldwell turned back to the *Saratoga* with two wounded crew members, Kenneth Bratton from Oxford, Mississippi, and Robert Morey of Los Angeles. Navy photographer Paul T. Barnett, of Corpus Christi, Texas, who went along to record the mission, was killed in the action. Bratton was struck in the legs and near the base of his spine by shell fragments but survived the flight back to the *Saratoga* by applying tourniquets to stem the flow of blood.[3]

Caldwell knew the plane's hydraulic system had been damaged and that only one landing gear was operable. He elected to land on the carrier rather than ditch in the sea because the seriously wounded Bratton might not be able to escape from the rear gun turret.

As Caldwell approached the carrier, he had one wheel down, no flaps, and no elevator controls. As he made a pass over the ship he held up two fingers for the land signal officer to show that he had two wounded aboard. The engine began to sputter, and the plane dipped almost into the water, but the engine caught just in time, and Caldwell went around for a final approach. As he came in, Caldwell kept the plane level and made a "fantastic" one-wheel landing, coming to a stop as the Avenger plowed into a barrier designed to stop careening aircraft.

"I'm ok, but I hurt like hell," Bratton said as the men began to pull him free.[4] Bratton survived and was evacuated to the States for medical treatment. His wife, Louise, recalled that "Kenny" was in a cast for some time

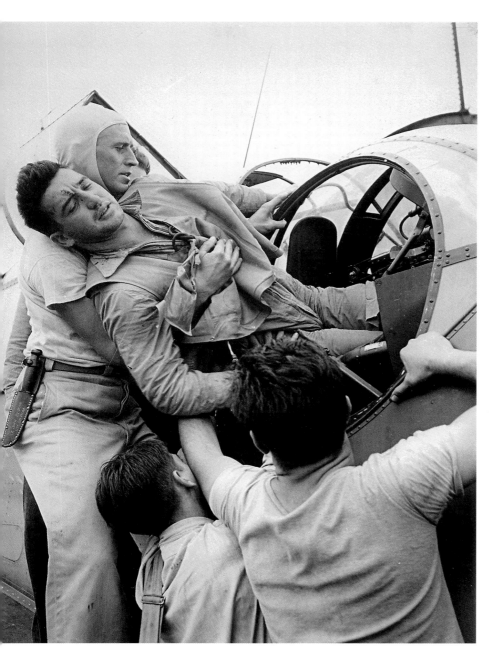

A wounded Kenny Bratton being removed from the turret gun of a navy Avenger torpedo bomber.

A corpsman awaiting the return of USS *Saratoga*'s planes from the Japanese naval base at Rabaul.

after being wounded. When he recuperated, he wanted to return to his old unit, but the navy refused to allow him back into combat.[5]

The photo ran in papers across the country and made Bratton a wartime celebrity. After recuperating in California, he was sent on war bond drives by the navy, appearing with Mary Martin, and was featured on Kate Smith's radio program.

After the war Bratton returned to Oxford, where he had grown up. His father had been a federal judge in Mississippi and Bratton had befriended and gone hunting with William Faulkner, the author, who lived nearby. Bratton attended the University of Mississippi for a year before volunteering for the navy.[6] When mustered out of the service, Bratton went to work for the Hill-Behan Lumber Company, which had outlets around the country. He never returned to college, and in 1961 he and Louise and their four children, two boys and two girls, moved to Covington, Louisiana.

"Everybody loved Kenny," said Louise, who remained in Covington. "He would do anything for you." He was a good old southern boy who loved to hunt and fish and was adored by all who met him. Bratton didn't talk much about the war and apparently wasn't badly affected by his wartime experiences and wounds. Occasionally his knee would lock up and he needed help to straighten it out. He had a steel plate in the knee and a depression near the base of his spine where he had been hit that day in November 1943. He always said that if the wound near his spine had been a fraction off, he would have been killed.[7]

Kenny Bratton died from colon cancer in 1983 at the age of sixty-two.

One of the men who pulled Bratton from the plane was navy lieutenant Julius "Julie" Bescos, behind Bratton and wearing a close-fitting carrier-deck cap.[8] Bescos, of Long Beach, California, was one of USC's earliest three-sport stars and was inducted into the USC Athletic Hall of Fame for earning nine letters in football (1932–34), basketball (1932–34), and baseball (1932 and 1934). He was a member of the unde-feated 1932 national championship football team and was the team's captain in 1934. He was also a skilled javelin thrower and golfer but did not have time to compete in those sports at USC.

Julio "Julie" Bescos later in life.

Following graduation Bescos joined the USC coaching staff in 1935, work-ing with the freshmen and junior varsity football, basketball, and baseball squads. He assisted the varsity football players from 1937 to 1941. He also was the men's head basketball coach in 1942, going 12–8 and finishing second in the league.

After the war he returned to USC but found it difficult to raise a family on coaching pay. Bescos joined StarKist foods, where he worked for forty years before retiring as national sales manager. He retired in 1978 to Long Beach, California, and served as president of the California and Southern

Navy photographer
Paul Barnett
preparing for his
last mission.

California Golf Association. He was ranked among the nation's top amateur golfers.[9] Bescos lived to be ninety-seven and died in 2009.

Bescos never saw Kenny Bratton again after pulling him from the plane, but he remembered him well. He said that Bratton would often come up on the flight deck while planes were being launched or landed and would stand right behind him. "He was a really nice guy," Bescos remembered.

There is an uncanny aspect to this story. Photographer Wayne Miller, who took the picture of Bratton's rescue, was assigned to fly on the Rabaul mission. The squadron photographer, Paul T. Barnett, had never flown in combat before and had received reassignment orders. The night before the mission, Barnett came to Miller and asked if he could go in his stead. Miller, who had traveled the world and seen his share of combat as a staff photographer for the great American photographer Edward Steichen, then in the navy, agreed. The mission cost Barnett his life.[10]

Roy Willis Humphrey Struggles for Life

Another poignant image of World War II, this photograph depicts a wounded soldier receiving a blood transfusion just behind the front lines in Agata, Sicily, the day that American and British forces landed on August 9, 1943. The Western Allies had swept the German and Italian forces out of North Africa and planned the conquest of Axis Italy by first invading Sicily.

The well-known critic of the time, Victor Keppler, called the photo "one of the greatest human interest shots to come from the war."[11] It depicts a grievously wounded American soldier and immediately begs the question, "Did this man survive?" The photograph, which received a 1944 Pulitzer Prize nomination, shows Third Infantry Division soldier Pvt. Roy Willis Humphrey, twenty-one, of Toledo, Ohio, receiving a blood transfusion administered by Pfc. Harvey White. John Stephen Wever took the shot. The photograph appeared in newspapers from coast to coast in the United States

Roy Humphry
at seventeen.

and was used by the Red Cross to encourage blood donations for the military. One of the newspapers that ran the photograph was the *Toledo Blade* in Humphrey's hometown. The *Blade* identified White, but Humphrey was identified only as a "wounded Yank." No one knew he was a local boy.[12]

Roy Humphrey died of his wounds on August 10, the day after the photo was taken. The *Blade* ran the photo on September 3, 1943, and ran a story about Humphrey's death four days later, on September 7, without ever connecting him to the soldier in the photograph.

Humphrey's obituary in the *Blade* began, "The mother of two sons will never hear from one of them again." The story stated that Humphrey was twenty-one, graduated from the Macomber Vocational Technical High School, and had worked as a welder in Toledo and Detroit. He volunteered for the paratroopers in 1942 before being transferred to the infantry. He joined the Third Division in North Africa in February 1943 while it was in training to make the Sicily landings.

The *Blade* article added that in letters to his mother, Humphrey said he was planning to return after the war, marry his sweetheart, get a job, and settle down. His mother never recovered from her son's death. "She really loved that kid," said Lee Weiser, who married Humphrey's sister, Winifred, shortly after Humphrey left for war. "I'm telling you, she was in bad shape after he was killed. She really missed him."[13]

Humphrey's body was returned to the United States in 1947 in a program to repatriate the war dead. He was buried in Toledo Memorial Park Cemetery.

Chapter 3

Talking Pike with Ike

It was a pivotal moment in history, June 5, 1944, the evening before the D-Day invasion of France. Thousands of American paratroopers from the 101st Airborne Division prepared for a night drop on the Normandy peninsula to confuse the Germans, seize strategic objectives, and clear the way for the landings at dawn the next morning. Shortly after this photograph was taken at a base in southern England, these paratroopers boarded hundreds of C-47 transports and flew into battle. They were among the first Allied soldiers to land in France, and they came in the dead of night, heralded by the drone of airplanes. They were to land in designated drop zones but were scattered across the Normandy peninsula, giving them an unexpected advantage over the Germans, who believed many thousands more paratroopers had landed. The saga of the 101st Airborne Division became lionized years later in Stephen Ambrose's *Band of Brothers.*

Long after the war, Wallace Strobel, the soldier pictured talking to General Dwight Eisenhower, "Ike," the Allied supreme commander in Europe, would occasionally wander into bookstores and tease his wife that he was going to look at his picture. Nevertheless, Strobel took his fame from the photograph in stride, and, in fact, he said it was "a little embarrassing."[1]

A native of Saginaw, Michigan, Strobel is the tall, blackened-faced Airborne lieutenant with the tag number 23 around his neck talking with Eisenhower while other paratroopers listen intently.

"It just happened to happen," Strobel said.[2] Ike had visited the 101st numerous times in the months before D-Day, and the men became used to the supreme commander being around. The day before the invasion was Strobel's twenty-second birthday, and he and his buddies prepared themselves for the coming night drop. They readied their equipment and blackened their faces to improve their chances of going undetected in the dark. At about 7 p.m., Eisenhower made a surprise visit to the division and chatted with the men as he went down a line of soldiers. Ike asked them if they were ready to go. When he got to Strobel he stopped and asked the young lieutenant about the fishing in Michigan, and an army photographer snapped several pictures. A short time later Eisenhower left, and the 101st boarded their

Supreme Allied Commander Dwight "Ike" Eisenhower chats with paratroopers, June 5, 1944, the night before they dropped into Normandy to start the D-Day invasion.

planes for the flight across the English Channel. The photo, released on June 7, became instantly famous and appeared in magazines and newspapers around the country.

It took Strobel some time to realize that he was in the foreground of the photograph. "I thought it was a poor picture, and I didn't know it was me at first," he said. Then he saw that the young officer had a tag around his neck stamped with the number 23. "That was my plane number and I thought, that's me!"[3]

He was the subject of numerous articles. History buffs sought his autograph, and he became friends with John Eisenhower, son of the former supreme commander. During the fortieth anniversary of D-Day, Strobel was invited to attend commemoration ceremonies in Normandy, where he stood near President Reagan. During observances for the fiftieth anniversary of D-Day, he was again one of the dignitaries. A likeness of the photograph appeared on a U.S. postage stamp commemorating Eisenhower that was issued in 1991. On the stamp Eisenhower was given a few more inches on his five-foot, nine-inch frame to make him the same height as Strobel.

Strobel said that his experiences during the D-Day invasion were less memorable than later action he and the 101st experienced in Holland and in Belgium during the Battle of the Bulge. He came out of the war without a scratch.

Strobel returned home, became president of Central Warehouse Inc., and was the cofounder of the First State Bank of Saginaw. He was also a chairman of the county GOP. He died August 27, 1999, in Saginaw at the age of seventy-seven.

Because of the famous image, the soldier in the center of the photograph, Sherman J. Oyler Jr., was also well known in Topeka, Kansas, where he settled after the war. Oyler, originally from Caldwell, Kansas, was wounded three times in the fighting in Normandy, Holland, and in Belgium during the Battle of the Bulge. Among the D-Day highlights, Oyler tells about meeting Eisenhower before leaving in a C-47 transport. "Eisenhower wanted to meet some soldiers from Kansas, so they shoved me and another man from Wichita to meet him," Oyler said. He admitted he was nervous and almost forgot his name.[4]

In another incident, Oyler jumped into a ditch to avoid mortar fire after a parachute landing in Holland later in the war. He tumbled on top of Walter Cronkite, then a CBS war correspondent. Hanging onto a portable typewriter and with patches on each shoulder saying "war correspondent," Cronkite said some things that you couldn't air on television. Oyler and two other soldiers in the ditch simply could not understand why anyone would be there who did not have to be. Years later Oyler wrote to Cronkite asking if he remembered the incident. Cronkite replied he remembered the ditch, although he didn't remember the names of the soldiers.

Oyler recalled the horrors of the Bulge in a 1994 newspaper interview. The 101st had been rushed to the town of Bastogne, where numerous roads intersected. It was a strategic point along the German advance route, and the Americans were determined to hold it at all costs. The men of the 101st were without adequate food, clothing, and ammunition and were surrounded for five days. Oyler recalled that the men couldn't dig in because the ground was so hard, so they often used the bodies of the dead as barriers. Wounded men froze to death, and the living scrounged for food in the cellars of abandoned houses.

Oyler said he always hated snow after the Bulge, but he returned to Kansas, where winter sets in with a vengeance. He received a bachelor's and a master's degree in education from Kansas State Teachers College in Emporia and taught in Topeka for twenty-five years. He also was a magistrate judge in Onaga.

On the anniversary of D-Day every year, Oyler would teach his students about World War II and the part he played as a paratrooper. He set up classroom displays of photographs, military patches, uniforms, and hardware for the students to see, and then, dressed in his old combat fatigues, he would demonstrate proper parachute landing procedure by jumping off his desk and landing on the floor.

Oyler married Joyce K. May, an Englishwoman he met while serving in Great Britain. They were married for fifty years before her death in 1997. The couple had a daughter. Sherman Oyler died at the age of seventy-eight in 1999.

Mary Doyle Keefe, model for *Rosie the Riveter*.

Rockwell's *Rosie the Riveter*

World War II forever changed American families and the social mores governing women. As millions of men went to war between 1941 and 1945, women took their place in the factories and arsenals all across the country. They turned out bullets and artillery shells, tanks and airplanes. They flew airplanes to bases around the country and the world to relieve men for combat duty. They got gritty and sweaty in the factories and on the farms, but they never relinquished their femininity, wearing lipstick and perfume as they always had.

In 1942 Americans began hearing about a defense worker named Rosie the Riveter in a popular song. Then posters appeared depicting women defense workers dressed in coveralls, bandannas covering their hair, and their hands and faces greasy from their work. They collectively became known as Rosie the Riveter and were personified in an illustration by Norman Rockwell.

Rockwell's Rosie appeared on the cover of the *Saturday Evening Post* on May 29, 1943. From then on the name Rosie the Riveter was imbedded in the American lexicon, and it resonates to this day.

Rockwell didn't draw Rosie from his imagination; he took her likeness—somewhat—from a model named Mary Doyle, a nineteen-year-old telephone operator in Arlington, Vermont, where Rockwell had his studio.[5] Arlington was a small town where everybody knew everybody, and everybody knew Rockwell. He asked Doyle to sit for him as the model for Rosie, and she accepted. She was happy to pick up a five-dollar sitting fee.

Doyle remembers arriving at the studio where Rockwell had assembled her costume, which originally included a white shirt and saddle shoes. She sat for several illustrations, all of which were destroyed when Rockwell's studio burned to the ground during the summer of 1943. She returned for a second session, when Rockwell decided he wanted her to wear a blue shirt and penny loafers.

Doyle first encountered Rockwell's depiction of her at a newsstand in Bennington, Vermont, where she saw his illustration on a poster advertising the May 29, 1943, edition of the *Saturday Evening Post*. She was shocked by the transformation of her slim figure into Rosie's muscular build, but Rockwell called and apologized for taking such liberties. Rockwell modeled his Rosie after Michelangelo's portrait of a beefy prophet Isaiah on the ceiling of the Vatican's Sistine Chapel.[6]

Rockwell's *Rosie the Riveter* became an iconic image. He portrayed her clad in overalls and a work shirt with the sleeves rolled up to reveal strong arms. Seated against the backdrop of an American flag and eating a sandwich, she had a riveting gun and a tin lunch box in her lap, and visor and goggles pushed back on her head. Despite her appearance, the work clothes, and the smudges on her arms and cheeks, Rosie's painted fingernails, lipstick, and her red curls convey her underlying femininity. As she eats, her feet are firmly planted on a copy of Adolf Hitler's *Mein Kampf*.

Mary Doyle went on to college and became a dental hygienist. She met her husband, Robert Keefe, when she cleaned his teeth. Robert is deceased, and Mary lived in retirement in Simsbury, Connecticut, where she died at ninety-four in 2015.

The five dollars a sitting that Doyle earned in 1943 can be contrasted with the nearly $5 million figure that Rockwell's original illustration of her brought in a 2002 Sotheby's auction in New York.

"One Never Knows What Tomorrow May Bring"

This full-page portrait of Lt. Jesse D. "Red" Franks first appeared in 1966 in the second volume of *The American Heritage Picture History of World War II* and was run opposite a photograph of film star James Stewart, who was a bomber pilot during the war.[7] Franks was a bombardier on the B-24 *Euroclydon,* and his photograph was undoubtedly given such good display because his image represented the ideal of the young American fighting man during the war—friendly, good looking, and slightly rumpled in comparison to the stern-looking and militarily correct Germans. Franks took part in Operation Tidal Wave, the horrific low-level American air raid against Ploesti, Romania, in which *Euroclydon* was one of three planes to lead the attack on August 1, 1943. The Romanian oil fields and refineries produced more than half of Nazi Germany's petroleum, and the Allies were determined to close down production.[8]

Lieutenant Franks, from Columbus, Mississippi, entered a Baptist seminary in Louisville, Kentucky, after college but dropped out in 1942 to join the Army Air Forces. His dream was to be a pilot, but he washed out of flight training and instead became an officer-bombardier. In 1943 *Euroclydon* was assigned to the Eighth Air Force in Great Britain and made several raids over occupied Europe. The bomb group was transferred to Libya to attack targets in Italy and prepare for the Ploesti raid.

One hundred and seventy-eight B-24s flew from Benghazi, over the Mediterranean, Albania, and Yugoslavia, to reach Ploesti. Because of a navigational error during the long flight, *Euroclydon* was

B-24s over the Ploesti, Romania, oil fields, August 1, 1943.

one of the first aircraft over the target and was shot down within minutes. A total of fifty-eight bombers were lost on the raid.

Franks was last seen bailing out from the burning plane. After that, nothing was heard from him, and the army at first told his father, Dr. Jesse D. Franks, a Baptist minister from Columbus, that Red was missing. They also told his fiancée, Dottie Turner. The young couple had met when they were in college in Jackson, Mississippi, and planned to marry after Dottie's graduation. With the coming of war they postponed their nuptials until Red came home.

The War Department later declared Red "killed in action." Dr. Franks, however, kept receiving reports that his son was alive and a POW, one from *Euroclydon*'s navigator, who was a prisoner of war, and one from the adjutant of Red's squadron. The government could provide no evidence to prove Red's death, even after the war ended. Dr. Franks never gave up hope that his son was alive and set out to find him. In 1947 he resigned his pastorate in Columbus to work in Geneva, Switzerland, where he could more easily continue the search. Like so many parents of the missing, Dr. Franks believed that his son could have been held captive by the Germans during the war and after war by the Russians, who eventually liberated Romania. He also worried that Red was suffering from amnesia from bailing out and was wandering about Eastern Europe. In 1948, however, after attempting to travel to Romania and scores of letters to congressmen and generals, Dr. Franks found his son. Red's body was finally identified. He had bailed out at too low an altitude and was killed instantly when he hit the ground a few miles beyond the Ploesti refineries. His body was then stripped of all identification by local Romanians, and his remains were buried in a private cemetery near Ploesti. When the war ended, U.S. Graves Registration personnel exhumed the bodies of scores of American fliers killed in raids on Ploesti. Red's body, still unidentified, was removed to Belgium, where it was interred in what is now the Ardennes American Cemetery among a group of unknown airmen. Only after continuous urgings by Dr. Franks and careful screening was Red's body finally identified.

It was later revealed by a surviving member of *Euroclydon*'s crew that Red died because he saved a comrade, Lt. Jack Warner, a good friend and the plane's navigator, who was seriously wounded. Warner said that the plane was engulfed in flame as it passed over Ploesti, and Red could have bailed out first and saved himself. Instead, Red helped the wounded Warner jump first, dragging him to the tiny nose-wheel escape hatch and pushing him out as the burning bomber lost altitude and was seconds away from crashing. By the time Red jumped the plane was too low. His parachute never opened. Jack Warner survived and died sixty years later.

The night before he died, Red wrote his father a letter that later appeared in the *Congressional Quarterly*. It is a testament to the strength and courage of this young American.

Dr. Franks said the loss of his son was the greatest tragedy of his life, but he was relieved that the uncertainty of not knowing if Red had lived or died was ended. He wrote, "I loved him more than life itself." Dottie Turner, Red's fiancée, never fully recovered from his death. In 1945 she married an Air Force officer.

Dr. Jesse D. Franks at the grave of his son at the Ardennes American Cemetery, 1949.

Dearest Dad:

I want to write you a little note before our big raid tomorrow. It will be the biggest and toughest we have had yet. Our target is the oil fields, which supply Germany with three-fourths of her oil. We will get our target at any cost, and on a raid we can never foresee all that will happen.

Our planes are made for high altitude bombing, but this time we are going in at 50 feet above our target, so there will be no second trip to complete the job. We will destroy the oil refineries in one blow. Hitler cannot run his planes, tanks and trucks without this oil, and the war will be

Jesse D. Franks, 1943.

shortened, they tell us, by a year after the raid, and may knock Italy clear out of the picture.

Dad, if anything happens — don't feel bitter at all. Please stay the same. I remember how happy you were when I decided to go to the Seminary, and then again, when I joined the Air Corps in preference to staying at the Seminary.

You are the best Dad in the world, and always too good to a boy who was a pretty bad little red-head at times.

I am glad I am in this group, and will get a chance at this important target. I know that it will save many lives from the results, so at any cost it is worth it. So, Dad, remember that, and the cost, whatever it may be, will not be in vain.

I don't want you to think that I gave up before I got into the air, no, that is not the reason I am writing this at all. We are fully aware of the danger of this raid, and I always want you to know that I love you, and am so proud to be your son, and can do this, even though my part is little.

Remember me to all the folks back home. Everyone has always gone out of their way to be nice to me. I love Columbus — everything about it — the people, town, and the spirit behind what makes it such a wonderful place to live. I love everything there.

Take good care of yourself, little Sis, and don't let this get you down, because I would never want it that way. Never change — be the same swell Dad always. Remember, you are doing the best job in the world now, and you always have done the best one.

Hope you don't get this letter, but one never knows what tomorrow may bring.

Your devoted son.[9]

Faris "Bob" Tuohy: Coffee after the Battle

This photograph was taken abroad the navy attack transport USS *Middleton* just after the Twenty-Second Marine Regiment returned from three days of operations against Engibi in the Eniwetok Atoll in the Marshall Islands. Eniwetok was assaulted and captured by the Americans as they advanced through the South and Central Pacific. The American strategy was to destroy important enemy bases that stretched from Japan to the Solomon Islands north of Australia. Each successive island victory brought the Americans closer to Japan.

Marine Pfc. Faris "Bob" Tuohy, nineteen, had no recollection of being photographed drinking a cup of coffee after the conquest of Engibi in February 1944.[10] The image appeared all over America as part of the effort to sell war bonds, and it was displayed in poster-size blowup in New York's Grand Central Station. Tuohy found out about the photo after his mother saw it weeks later and wrote him that it had appeared back home.

"The fight on Engebi was real sharp," Tuohy recalled, adding that it was a good place for the Twenty-Second Marine Regiment to be battle tested. The three men, exhausted and grimy, Tuohy, Steve Garboski, right, and Jack Delaney, center, were taking a coffee break in the ship's galley.

"We were terribly sunburned when the picture was taken," Tuohy added. "Engebi was a white sand island, and the water was so blue and the sun was so intense that even the inside of my nose was sunburned." As for the dirt and grease on his body, Tuohy remarked, "It's a funny thing. That just gets on you when you're doing that kind of work. No blood, just grime." It took the regiment three days to take the island.

The fight for Eniwetok wasn't over. The next day Tuohy and the Twenty-Second Marines were sent to take Parry Island, another objective in the atoll. In that fight Tuohy was slightly wounded. By the end of the campaign, the

Twenty-Second had landed on four different islands at Eniwetok to clear them of Japanese troops.

After Eniwetok was secured, the Twenty-Second Marines were shipped back to Guadalcanal to train for the invasion of Guam. The trip to Guam was an ordeal; the Marines boarded naval transports, this time an LST, and were housed on the deck for the fifty-four-day voyage. "We were dirty, there were no beds, and no provisions to wash," Tuohy said. Part of the trip was spent circling in the Central Pacific as the top brass waited to determine if the Twenty-Second was needed to assist in the invasion of Saipan in the Marianas island chain.

Tuohy fought on Guam, after which the Twenty-Second Marines were again shipped back to Guadalcanal to train for the invasion of Okinawa. The Twenty-Second was merged then with two other "independent" Marine regiments, the Fourth and the Twenty-Ninth, to form the Sixth Marine Division. Tuohy survived Okinawa with a "scratch."

At war's end Tuohy was shipped to China. "We went up to Shandong Province and took the surrender of a Japanese army in Qingdao. It was quite a city, lots of stone buildings, world renowned for their cookery, and it was said to be the home of Confucius. I was stationed there from September of 1945 to the spring of 1946."

Tuohy broke a foot in an accident while in China and was flown to a hospital ship in Shanghai. "I was a 'regular Marine,' so they could do what they wanted to with me — they didn't have to pay attention to a point system for regulars, and I was upset because I had the points to get out. But in retrospect I'm glad. China was a fascinating place."

Tuohy married his sweetheart in 1947, and the couple had three children — two daughters and a son. Tuohy became vice president for land development for the American Metals Company, which later was merged into the Phelps Dodge Corporation. After living in many parts of the country, he retired to Lakeland, Florida. He now lives in Columbus, Ohio.

What became of the other two men in the photograph? Steve Garboski, right, was killed on Guam by friendly fire from U.S. aircraft bombing Japanese positions. Tuohy witnessed the battered body of his comrade and after the war visited Garboski's parents, who were living near Flemington, New Jersey, where Garboski was later buried. Jack Delaney, or a Marine Tuohy

Faris Tuohy
in 2006.

believes was Jack Delaney, center, was killed on Okinawa. Tuohy was the
lone survivor.

Faris Tuohy penned a short note to the author about his comrades who
died in the war; it was on a sticky note attached to the back of his letter.

He reflected in 2014, at age ninety, on his war experiences. "My military
history is now seventy years [ago], and my little poem is still so very real,
brings a little moist eyes just writing about it."

When I was young,
And in those far off killing times,
Companions lost to the enemy were easier to accept then.
Now, when here, in the steep
Downhill of a long and lucky life
As their faces fade and
Their names are almost gone
I mourn them every day.[11]
8/18/06

Chapter 4

Future Dodger Hits the Beach

The American public rarely saw photographs during the war of Americans killed in action or soldiers in combat the instant they were wounded, so this photograph of two Marines sinking to their knees seconds after being hit on a beach on the Pacific island of Saipan was highly unusual. According to the caption, the two were hit by sniper fire as they landed with their unit.

Saipan, assaulted on June 15, 1944, along with its sister islands of Guam and Tinian, in the Marianas, was an important strategic objective. The proximity of the island chain to Japan permitted American B-29 "Superforts" to engage in a constant bombing campaign against the Japanese homeland. The *Enola Gay,* the B-29 that dropped the atomic bomb on Hiroshima, took off from Tinian a year later in 1945.

The two men, pictured at the moment they were hit, were from the Second Armored Amphibian Battalion, which was attached to the Second Marine Division. The battalion was formed to lead the assault on key islands in the South Pacific. They fought at Saipan, Tinian, and Iwo Jima and were preparing for new battles when the war ended.

What happened to the two Marines? Did they survive?

No one knows, not even the Marine in the center of the photograph looking toward the camera. His name is Wayne Terwilliger, and to those who follow baseball, he became well known as he went on to play for five different major league teams over a nine-year period.[1] He was also a part of eleven minor league teams and spent twelve years as a coach in the major leagues, receiving World Series rings while coaching for the Minnesota Twins in 1987 and 1991.

Terwilliger began his career with the Chicago Cubs in 1949 and was later traded to the Brooklyn Dodgers in 1951. He was a second baseman and once substituted for the great Jackie Robinson when Robinson was out with an injury. During the game, Terwilliger made a spectacular save, and Robinson approached him to say, "I couldn't have made that play."[2]

Terwilliger was eighteen when the photograph was taken on Saipan's "Green Beach." "I recognized the one Marine facing the camera as me," Terwilliger recalled. "I was the only one I can remember with rolled-up

Marine Wayne Terwilliger, face to the camera, landing on Saipan, 1944.

sleeves, a canteen on each hip, and always wore my helmet unstrapped. The Marines without the backpack are tank men, the ones with the backpack are infantry Marines. The second Marine from the right looks like Simon P. Miller, who was a tank man."[3]

He did not know the two men who were hit. Everything was happening too fast; the men were under fire and racing for cover. "I do not know if anybody was hit. . . . I know I ducked at the right time when the mortars were coming."[4]

Terwilliger was a tank radioman and machine gunner. Of his war experiences he says tersely, "Never wounded."[5]

After his major league career, Terwilliger managed the Fort Worth Cats and at age eighty had logged more time in professional baseball — fifty-six years — than anyone else. At eighty, Terwilliger felt much younger and decided to keep on coaching. When he announced plans to retire, he told his wife he would just hang around the house. She exclaimed: "Hang around the house? *You?*"[6] So rather than manage the Cats, Terwilliger agreed to sign on for another stint as first-base coach. After his coaching days with the Cats, Terwilliger took up bagging at a local grocery store. He is eighty-eight years old.

The photograph was well enough known that it was later used as a backdrop for the Postal Service when it issued stamps in the 1940s related to World War II.

A Chance Encounter in Paris

Why would a respectable woman approach and hug a dirty, grimy American soldier whom she had never met? Because Paris, after four years of Nazi occupation, had just been liberated, and Parisians were joyously celebrating their newfound freedom from tyranny. After the Allies landed at Normandy on June 6, 1944, expectant Parisians waited anxiously as the Americans and British fought their way through stiff German resistance. Finally, the German Seventh Army collapsed, and the way to Paris was open. Thousands of American troops poured into the city in the days after August 25, and wild celebrations followed.

Sgt. Kenneth
Averill during the
liberation of Paris,
August 1944.

Kenneth Averill, a twenty-six-year-old sergeant from Hazel Park, Michigan, arrived in Paris that day as a member of an army Signal Corps unit.[7] He had landed with the Fourth Division at Utah Beach the afternoon of D-Day, and commanded a team of radio operators that was responsible for maintaining communications between division headquarters and the division's Twelfth Infantry Regiment.

A fellow Signal Corps photographer photographed the six-foot, two-inch Averill as a happy Frenchwoman approached and began hugging him when his unit passed by some government buildings about a mile from Notre Dame cathedral. Newspapers around the United States picked up the photograph and gave it prominent display.

Averill spent two days in Paris. The first night his unit bedded down in a garage, and the next night they slept in a park on the city's outskirts. The division then marched on to fight in some of the major battles in the remaining months of the war, but Averill had only one close call, when a bullet pierced his helmet.

After the war, Averill returned to Michigan and worked for a beverage concern for forty years before retiring and making his home in Troy, Michigan, with his wife. The Averills have two children.

Did he ever again hear from the woman who hugged him that afternoon in Paris in 1944? No, Averill says. "All the girls came out. They were just grabbing any GI and hugging them. It's an event I will never forget."

Memphis Belle

The *Memphis Belle* was the B-17 that brought the air war in Europe home to the American public when in May 1943 it was one of the first England-based bombers to complete twenty-five missions over occupied Europe and Germany. Twenty-five missions was the magic number, and in the early years of the war few airmen survived to make that many.

The *Memphis Belle* also became famous because it was featured in the documentary *Memphis Belle: A Story of a Flying Fortress,* produced and released in 1944 by director William Wyler. The documentary showed the air war up close, deadly and at twenty-five thousand feet above the checkered green-and-brown landscape of Nazi Germany. Wilder and his cameramen accompanied the *Belle* on bombing missions and shot dramatic footage from a raid on Wilhelmshaven, Germany, showing B-17s flying through walls of flak and German fighter planes zooming in for the kill with their cannons blinking as they take aim on the bomber formation. B-17s are filmed going down in death spirals after being hit, while racks of bombs lazily fall on the target below from the *Belle*'s bomb bay.

The *Memphis Belle* was assigned to the Eighth Bomber Command and arrived in England in September 1942, to join the Ninety-First Bomb Group

The *Memphis Belle* restored at the Museum of the United States Air Force.

at Bassingbourn. These were dark days for Bomber Command, as the American Air Forces were learning how to fight. The *Memphis Belle* flew mostly missions against German facilities in France and a few to targets in western Germany. Its last mission was on May 20, 1943, to Wilhelmshaven, to attack submarine and harbor facilities. Normally the crew would have been assigned to new duties and the plane left to continue on bombing missions, but crew and plane were shipped back to the States for a war bond tour.

The *Memphis Belle* was named for pilot Capt. Robert Morgan's sweetheart at the time, Margaret Polk. While she and Morgan never married, she remained an honorary member of the Memphis Belle Association and helped fund-raising for it until she died in 1990.

After the war, the *Memphis Belle* began a checkered career. Reclaimed from an airplane graveyard in Oklahoma, the aircraft was purchased for $350 by the city of Memphis, where after several years in storage it was displayed at a National Guard armory and exposed to the elements along with souvenir hunters, who stripped most of its interior. In 2004 it was disassembled and shipped to the National Museum of the United States Air Force in Dayton, Ohio, where it has been restored and is now on display.[8]

Life and Death of *Wee Willie*

World War II was a killing ground for aircraft as well as for men. Hundreds of thousands of American planes swarmed in the skies all around the world. The Army Air Forces alone acquired 231,099 planes of all types, 12,692 of which were B-17s, the famous bombers better known as the Flying Fortress. Its rival in the skies was the B-24 Liberator, of which 18,190 were manufactured. While the United States produced huge numbers of aircraft, tens of thousands were lost as a result of enemy action or accidents, and thousands of B-17s were shot down over occupied Europe and Germany.

Sixty planes, mostly B-17s, were shot down on one horrendous raid against ball-bearing works in the city of Schweinfurt, Germany, representing about 26 percent of the attacking force. Sixty planes down represents almost six hundred airman killed, wounded, or captured, not to mention the dead and wounded in the planes that made it back to bases in England. Nearly

Crew of the B-17
Wee Willie.

two-thirds of the attacking force of 178 B-24s were shot down or damaged beyond repair in the August 1, 1943, low-level attack on the Ploesti, Romania, oil fields and refineries.

Histories of the war are not complete without photographs of vast fleets of these four-engine bombers from the Eighth Air Force based in England, and the Fifteenth Air Force based in southern Italy, winging their way to enemy targets. One is prompted to ask how many of those planes survived those missions, let alone the war. Undoubtedly most were shot down, wrecked in an accident, or damaged so badly that they were scavenged for spare parts.

One wonders about photographs of aircrews like the one above that flew in the B-17 *Wee Willie.* How many of those kneeling, smiling young men, some as young as eighteen, with their lives ahead of them, were killed, wounded, or taken prisoner after bailing out. In the first years of the war—1942 and 1943—an air crewman had only a 25 percent chance of completing his twenty-

The *Wee Willie* going down over Germany.

five-mission tour of duty. Only later in the war did the survival figures improve in conjunction with the arrival of the long-range P-51 fighter plane that could accompany the bombers all the way to Berlin. The Mustangs, as the P-51s were named, provided a protective screen around the bombers and fended off attacks by German fighter planes.

Wee Willie was a veteran of the bombing campaign against Germany, flying 128 missions over the continent until April 1945. The war was almost over. On April 8 *Wee Willie* flew with 322 Squadron, Ninety-First Bomb Group, stationed at Bassingbourn, on a mission over Germany. That was the day the plane's luck ran out. *Wee Willie* took a direct hit from flak over Stendal, Saxony-Anhalt, Germany. A gunner in a nearby squadron related the final moments in an after-action report.

"I observed [the bomber] receive a direct flak hit approximately between the bomb bay and the No. 2 [inboard motor on the left wing] engine. The aircraft immediately started into a vertical dive. The aircraft fuselage was on fire and when it had dropped approximately 5,000 feet the left wing fell off. It continued down and when the fuselage was about 3,000 feet from the ground it exploded, and then exploded again when it hit the ground. I saw no crew members leave the aircraft or parachutes."

But two crew members did survive: the pilot, Lt. Robert Fuller of Hollywood, California, and tail gunner, Sgt. Lemoyne Miller of Butler, Pennsylvania. The rest perished with the plane.

Were any of the men in the photo above on *Wee Willie* when the plane went down? It's difficult to say. Crews changed every day, as did the planes, so the chances are that on *Wee Willie*'s death ride she was manned by crew members other than the ones in this photo. The photo of *Wee Willie* falling in pieces was taken on that fateful day of April 8, 1945, from the bomb camera of a nearby B-17, a month, exactly, before the war ended. Were it not for this image, *Wee Willie*'s name would have disappeared into obscurity.[9]

Rose of York

When this shiny new B-17 arrived at the Eighth Air Force base at Thurleigh in Bedfordshire, England, on May 5, 1944, she was named by her crew in honor of the future queen of England, and her name was painted in bold red letters on the plane's nose.[10] The *Princess Elizabeth* flew several missions over Europe before orders came down to delete the name Elizabeth. King George VI, her father, feared that if the plane were shot down, the Germans would be handed a propaganda coup. Crew from the B-17 "Murder Incorporated" were captured, and the Germans claimed that the American bombing campaign was an international criminal act orchestrated by gangsters. Henceforth, the *Princess Elizabeth* was dubbed *The Princess,* and she flew additional missions over Europe, including a June 21 raid on Berlin. A crew member suggested that the real Princess Elizabeth, who was planning a visit to Thurleigh, christen the plane and rename it for her.

King George picked a new name for the plane, *Rose of York,* and the name was printed in bold letters on both sides of the nose, along with a white rose, symbol of the House of York. Princess Elizabeth arrived at Thurleigh on July 6, 1944, and christened the plane.

Would Princess Elizabeth's karma protect the *Rose of York?* It would appear that it did, for the plane flew another fifty missions, bringing the total number to more than one hundred. Then she flew on February 3, 1945, against Berlin. A BBC reporter, Guy Byam, flew with the crew to record the sounds of a bombing raid over Germany with a newly devised "midget"

Crew of the B-17 *Rose of York* greeting the future queen Elizabeth.

tape recorder, the type that became commonplace years later. Byam was a courageous reporter who had been invalided out of the Royal Navy after being wounded. He had flown on Royal Air Force bombing missions and jumped with paratroopers into Normandy during the D-Day invasion and with British paratroopers into Holland at Arnhem.

The *Rose of York* made it to Berlin, where she was badly shot up, and began limping home to Thurleigh. The pilot, Capt. Vernon Daley, radioed as the *Rose of York* reached the North Sea coast, reporting that two engines were out but that he had control of the aircraft. That was the last transmission, and the plane, along with her crew and Byam, disappeared without a trace. The *Rose of York* now lies somewhere beneath the waves.

Chapter 5

"Maybe Joe needs a rest. He's talkin' in his sleep."

Bill Mauldin and Willie and Joe

Bill Mauldin's cartoon characters, infantrymen Willie and Joe, were the most beloved soldiers of World War II. These two scruffy, exhausted, yet observant GIs served throughout the European theater, reflecting on the ironies and absurdities of the war. They, or Mauldin, lampooned the brass so accurately that Gen. George Patton threatened to throw Mauldin in the stockade for insubordination. In one cartoon a desk-bound shavetail (a green lieutenant), neatly dressed in clean, well-pressed fatigues, bellows at dirty, unshaven infantrymen, just back from the front lines, to look smart and shape up. In another, spit-and-polish generals standing in a circle lament the military bearing of nearby rumpled, dirty, and exhausted infantrymen fresh from battle. Willie made the cover of *Time* in the June 18, 1945, issue.[1]

Mauldin, from Mountain Peak, New Mexico, was a friend of the "dog-faces," or lowly GIs of the war, because he had been one himself. He joined the Oklahoma National Guard—Forty-Fifth Division—before the war and experienced army life as a private. To avoid the dullness and routine of barracks life, he volunteered to work on the division newspaper. Overseas this eventually led to his being allowed to roam all over the battlefields, producing a variety of cartoons for the army newspaper, *Stars and Stripes.* He would mingle with front-line troops and was wounded in the shoulder by German mortar fire while visiting a machine gun crew near Monte Cassino in Italy.

By war's end he was a sergeant with his own jeep and a job so important for the morale of the troops that when Patton threatened him with jail, the supreme Allied commander, General Eisenhower, intervened and told Patton to leave Mauldin alone because his cartoons gave the soldiers an outlet for their frustrations. Mauldin told an interviewer later, "I always admired Patton. Oh, sure, the stupid bastard was crazy. He was insane. He thought he was living in the Dark Ages. Soldiers were peasants to him. I didn't like that attitude, but I certainly respected his theories and the techniques he used to get his men out of their foxholes."[2]

By the end of the war Mauldin received the army's Legion of Merit for his cartoons. In 1945, at the age of twenty-three, he won the Pulitzer Prize, and the first civilian publication of his World War II work, *Up Front,* was a

Willie and Joe appeared in *Stars and Stripes*, the army newspaper printed in the various theaters of operation during World War II. This was one of hundreds of such cartoons produced by Bill Mauldin, and Willie and Joe became favorites of American GIs.

Bill Mauldin during
World War II.

best seller. The cartoons are interwoven with an impassioned telling of his
observations of war.

After the war, Mauldin turned to drawing political cartoons, many of
which were not well received by newspaper editors, who were hoping for
more apolitical Willie and Joe cartoons. But Mauldin's attempt to carry
Willie and Joe into civilian life was unsuccessful.

In 1959, Mauldin won another Pulitzer Prize for a cartoon depicting *Doctor
Zhivago* author Boris Pasternak in a Soviet gulag with the caption, "I won
the Nobel Prize for literature. What was your crime?"

Mauldin wanted to have Willie and Joe killed on the last day of combat,
but *Stars and Stripes* dissuaded him. He drew his famous characters only
a few times after the war: for the funerals of Generals Omar Bradley and

George C. Marshall, both of whom he considered "soldiers' generals"; for a *Life* magazine article on the "New Army"; and to memorialize fellow cartoonist Milton Caniff.

Mauldin died in 2003, from complications of Alzheimer's disease. He is buried in Arlington National Cemetery. He was eighty-one. In 2010, the United States Post Office released a first-class denomination (then forty-four cents) postage stamp in Mauldin's honor, depicting him with Willie and Joe.

Earl Leidner: A Face on a Stamp

Like the men of the army's Twenty-Eighth Division, Earl Leidner was given an honor in 1945 rarely bestowed on a living American. His face appeared on a U.S. postage stamp when he was only twenty-one.[3] Leidner appeared with several anonymous sailors on the three-cent stamp commemorating the U.S. Navy. Each branch of the military was honored by commemorative stamps at the end of World War II, including one depicting the Twenty-Eighth Division marching down the Champs-Élysées in Paris.

Leidner's path to the postage stamp was serendipitous. The Allentown, Pennsylvania, native was working at Bethlehem Steel when he enlisted in the navy in 1942 at age eighteen. While at the Great Lakes Naval Training Center, he and several other recruits were told to don their whites, line up in a field, and smile at a camera.

Earl Leidner, front row, left, above the word "united."

There was no explanation given for the photo session. But unexplained orders were common, and Leidner never asked why. It wasn't until three years later that a buddy told him that the photograph was used for the commemorative stamp. And it wasn't until 1947, when Leidner was in San Francisco, having completed his service in the navy, that he first saw the three-cent stamp. He was pictured in the front of a group, right next to the three-cent symbol, smiling brightly. "I didn't think much about it," Leidner said in an interview in 1999. "I had other things on my mind. We were home safe, and the war was over."

"What's a stamp? There were millions of them," he said. He saved one of the stamps as a souvenir, and then forgot about it for many years.

His wife, Grace, whom he met in 1973, was shocked that Leidner took the honor so lightly. "I gave him a new wallet to replace one that was worn out," she said. When he emptied the old one I saw a stamp that was crumpled almost beyond recognition. He had never mentioned it. When I saw what it was, I went on a quest to get a good one."

"When I told stamp dealers why I wanted it—that there was a picture of my husband on it—they didn't believe me, saying that you had to be dead to get your face on a stamp. I told him my husband was very much alive." A friend who collects stamps got the Leidners a block of four.

During his time in the service, Leidner was first an instructor in antiaircraft gunnery. He spent the rest of the war—twenty-six months—on the USS *Vincennes,* a light cruiser. As a gunner's mate, Leidner manned the antiaircraft guns, and toward the war's end he and his comrades faced Japanese kamikaze suicide planes off the coast of Japan. "Two or three times a week the kamikazes would attack, usually at night," Leidner said. "They dropped flares that were so bright you could read a newspaper by their light and that illuminated the entire task force." Leidner remembers the planes coming in so close "I could see their eyes just before they died."

After the war Leidner worked at Bell of Pennsylvania as an outside plant engineer until his retirement in 1979. He was a resident of Easton, Pennsylvania, when he died in June 1999.

On a Wing and a Prayer

The Boeing Aircraft Company during World War II advertised its B-17s as made to withstand terrific punishment. The claim rang true in early 1943 when the B-17 the *All American* survived a midair collision with an enemy fighter plane and managed to return to base in Algeria with its entire crew

unharmed. The plane was piloted by Kendrick R. "Sonny" Bragg, who first flew missions over Europe and was later transferred to North Africa.[4]

The *All American* was on a mission to Bizerta, Tunisia, on February 1, 1943, on what was expected to be a "milk run"—an easy assignment—but it turned out to be anything but. The *All American* and its wingman (the aircraft flying beside it in formation) dodged flak over the target, and as they pulled away on a clear, almost cloudless day, two German Messerschmitt fighters—Bf 109s—were following.

The B-17 *All American* struggling to make it back to base in Tunisia, 1943.

Kendrick Bragg.

The damage,
close up.

Suddenly the enemy planes moved in for an attack, two small specks at first that got larger and larger as they maneuvered for a frontal attack. The Germans had discovered that B-17s were most vulnerable from the front. "On they came," Bragg said, "one plane about thirty seconds behind the other. They were ready for a one-two punch with their terrific firing power."[5]

Bragg began a slight dive as the B-17s and the Bf 109s opened fire, sending brilliant tracer bullets flying in both directions. Bragg's wingman started smoking and drifted downward in an uncontrolled spiral. The second enemy fighter took aim and followed the leader into a roll, as the *All American*'s guns ripped into the plane. The Bf 109 streaked on toward the *All American*, and Bragg rammed the stick forward in a violent attempt to avoid collision. "The rate of closure of the two planes was close to 600 miles-an-hour and my action seemed sluggish. I flinched as the fighter passed inches over my head and then I felt a slight thud like a coughing engine. I checked the engines and the controls. The trim tabs were not working. I tried to level the All American but she insisted on climbing. It was only with the pressure from knees and hands that I was able to hold her in anything like a straight line. By throttling back the engines we could keep her on a fairly even keel."[6]

The *All American* was at twelve thousand feet as Bragg left the cockpit and was stunned when he looked back into the fuselage. "A torn mass of shredded metal greeted my eyes. Wires were dangling, and sheets of metal were flapping as the air rushed in through the torn wreckage. The enemy fighter had cut completely through three-fourths of the plane, and a large piece of the Bf 109's wing was lodged in the tail of our plane. It left our tail section hanging on by a few slender spars and a narrow strip of metallic skin."

Bragg climbed into the upper turret to assess the damage from the outside and discovered that the tail section was swinging as much as a foot and a half out of line with the front of the plane. To make matters worse, the left horizontal stabilizer was missing, explaining why the airplane was so difficult to handle.

Bragg decided to head back to the base at Biskra and ordered everyone to be ready to bail out. "As we neared the field we fired three emergency flares, then circled at 2,000 feet while the other planes cleared the runways. We could see the alert crews, ambulances, and crash trucks making ready for us."

Without radio contact, Bragg had to wait for the signal that all was clear.

A green flare shot up from the field, and Bragg lowered the landing gear and flaps to test the reaction of the *All American*. They worked. Bragg had two alternatives: attempt a landing, or bail out over the field and let the plane fly alone until she crashed—always a dangerous thing to do. He chose to land. "She had brought us safely through so far; I knew she would complete the mission. The crew decided to ride her down too."

Bragg made a long, careful approach to the strip with partial power, until the front wheels touched. He cut the throttles and pushed the stick forward to hold the tail section high until it eased down of its own weight as it lost speed.

Bragg noted: "I could feel the grating as she dragged without tail wheel along the desert sands. She came to a stop and I ordered the copilot to cut the engines. We were home."[7]

Bragg was born in Savannah and graduated from Savannah High School, where he was class president, student commanding officer of the ROTC, captain of the football and basketball teams, and undefeated springboard diving champion. He attended Duke University and played on the 1938 Rose Bowl Team. Following the war, Bragg graduated from Princeton University with a degree in architecture. He worked in New Jersey, in Puerto Rico, and then moved to St. Thomas, the Virgin Islands, where he practiced architecture for thirty years. He died in 1999 at age eighty-one.

Nuts!

It was Brig. Gen. Anthony McAuliffe who immortalized the retort, "Nuts!" in reply to the German commander who demanded that McAuliffe surrender the 101st Airborne Division defending Bastogne during the Battle of the Bulge. The "Screaming Eagles" had been rushed to Bastogne to hold the crossroads town to stop the German advance to reach the Meuse River, split the American and British armies, and capture the port of Antwerp, which supplied the advancing Allies. Surrounded and running low on supplies, the men of the 101st dug in and doggedly fought off repeated enemy attacks, thus the moniker: "the Battered Bastards of Bastogne."[8]

At noon on December 22, men from Company F were astonished to see four Germans, two officers and two enlisted men, appear in front of their

Gen. Anthony
McAuliffe.

positions carrying a white flag. The enemy soldiers also carried a surrender
ultimatum and asked to speak to the Americans' "commanding general."
The message read:

> To the U.S.A. Commander of the encircled town of Bastogne.
>
> The fortune of war is changing. This time the U.S.A. forces in and near
> Bastogne have been encircled by strong German armored units. More
> German armored units have crossed the river Our near Ortheuville, have
> taken Marche and reached St. Hubert by passing through Hompre-Sibret-
> Tillet. Libramont is in German hands.
>
> There is only one possibility to save the encircled U.S.A. troops from
> total annihilation: that is the honorable surrender of the encircled town. In
> order to think it over a term of two hours will be granted beginning with
> the presentation of this note.
>
> If this proposal should be rejected one German Artillery Corps and six

heavy A.A. Battalions are ready to annihilate the U.S.A. troops in and near Bastogne. The order for firing will be given immediately after this two hours' term.

General McAuliffe, normally the assistant division commander, was the acting division commander in the absence of Maj. Gen. Maxwell Taylor, who was away in Washington. Holed up in a cellar headquarters to escape constant enemy artillery fire, McAuliffe was informed of the two-hour demand by his chief of staff, Lt. Col. Ned Moore.

"What does it say, Ned?" McAuliffe asked.

"They want you to surrender," Moore said.

"Aw, nuts!" McAuliffe said.

When McAuliffe sat down to respond to the Germans in writing, he was at a loss for words.

"That crack you made would be hard to beat," said McAuliffe's aide, Harry Kinnard.

"What was that?" McAuliffe asked.

"Nuts!

The Germans were perplexed by what the word meant, but the word "nuts" and General McAuliffe became immortalized in the lexicon of World War II history.

McAuliffe was born in 1898 and was forty-six when he said the word that made him famous. Born in Washington, D.C., he attended West Virginia University in 1916–17 and graduated from West Point in 1918, commissioned as a second lieutenant.

During the invasion of Normandy, he was commander of artillery for the 101st. He later fought with the division in Holland, where he went into battle in a glider.

After the Bulge, McAuliffe was given command of the 103rd Infantry Division until the end of the war in Europe. Following the war he was variously head of Army Personnel, and commander in chief of the U.S. Army in Europe in 1955. Retiring from the army in 1956, he worked for American Cyanamid Corporation and lived in Chevy Chase, Maryland, until his death on August 11, 1975. He is buried with his wife and son in Arlington National Cemetery.

Lt. Robert Hite, Doolittle Raider

Texas-born Lt. Robert Hite, twenty-two, found himself a prisoner of the Japanese in April 1942 after he and his crew bailed out of their B-25 Mitchell bomber over enemy-occupied China. He was the copilot of *Bat out of Hell*, one of sixteen bombers that lifted off the aircraft carrier *Hornet* on April 18, 1942, to bomb the Japanese home islands in what is now known as "the Doolittle Raid."[9] The bombardment was in retaliation for the Japanese attack on Pearl Harbor, but could be only a symbolic one. The Americans didn't have the military might to strike a crippling blow. But the Japanese could be certain afterward that the Americans would be coming in vastly greater numbers to attack Japan as the war progressed.

Bat out of Hell made her bomb run and succeeded in reaching China, where all the Doolittle raiders were directed to land in Chinese territory

left Capt. Robert Hite during World War II.

right Lt. Col. Robert Hite, retired.

not occupied by the Japanese, but the plane ran out of gas. Hite was held prisoner for three years, much of it in solitary confinement. Other members of his crew, Lt. William Farrow, the pilot, of Darlington, South Carolina, and Sgt. Harold Spatz, twenty-one, of Lebo, Kansas, were executed by the Japanese as "war criminals" for allegedly killing innocent civilians.

Hite survived the war, and after recovering from his ordeal he stayed in the Air Force until 1955, when he went into the hotel business in Camden, Arkansas, and Enid, Oklahoma. His wife, Portia, died in 1998, and he later married Dottie Fitzhugh, widow of Lt. William N. Fitzhugh, copilot in the second B-25 to take off from the *Hornet,* just after Col. Jimmy Doolittle lifted off the carrier. Hite lived in Camden, Arkansas, and died in 2015.

Chapter 6

The Dangers of Carrier Landings

Flying from aircraft carriers has always been a hazardous endeavor, and flying into combat adds to the danger. Pilots used as much of the flight deck as possible for takeoff early in World War II. Still, if anything failed, the plane might crash into the sea and be sliced in two by the oncoming bow of the ship. Later, planes were launched into the air by hydraulic catapults that improved takeoff performance.

On landing, pilots had to hit a postage stamp that pitched and rolled in the sea, and had to concentrate on the antics of the land signal officer who directed the plane in for a landing with brightly colored hand-held paddles while standing on a small platform adjacent to and at the rear of the flight deck. If the left wing was too low, the right paddle would be dipped down low, and the signal officer often danced a ballet at the back of the flight deck, directing the planes home.

If a plane was cleared to land, the pilot had to hit the deck just right so that the arrester hook on the plane's tail grabbed one of the steel cables stretched across the rear of the flight deck. If the plane missed, it either tried to regain altitude and make another landing attempt, or it went careening up the deck, to be stopped by a heavy net barrier. All in all, landing on a carrier could be a harrowing experience, and many planes crashed.

Ensign John George Fraifogl had made a perfect landing on the USS *Ticonderoga* on July 1, 1944, when things went wrong.[1] The belly gasoline tank slung under the fuselage to give fighter planes greater range was knocked loose from the jolt of landing and bounced underneath the spinning propeller. Instantly, the F6F Hellcat fighter was engulfed in flame, and Fraifogl threw himself from the cockpit to escape the inferno. He injured his back and knee during his hurried exit but was otherwise unhurt.

Ensign John George Fraifogl bails out of his burning Hellcat navy fighter, 1944.

Fraifogl joined the navy in 1941 and became a pilot after training at Pensacola Naval Base, Florida, and was commissioned there in 1943. During his stint in the navy he also served as a flight instructor and test pilot. He married his sweetheart, Minnie, the same day he was commissioned.

After the war Fraifogl returned to Mansfield, Ohio, about fifteen miles from his birthplace in Crestline, Ohio, and became manager of office services for the Tappan Company. He and Minnie had three children, including twins. The couple had been married sixty years when Fraifogl died at the age of eighty-three in 2003. Minnie died in 2009 at age eighty-seven.

Fraifogl flew many missions against the Japanese and survived unhurt. In fact, flying may have saved his life. While he was on a mission, the *Ticonderoga* was attacked and bombed by enemy planes. When Fraifogl returned to his ship, he found that big chunks of shrapnel had penetrated his quarters and smashed into his bed.[2]

Nursing the Wounded

It was a man's war, but when soldiers were wounded, it was often the women who took care of them. Evangeline Coeyman, an army nurse, was attached to the Fifty-Ninth Field Hospital that followed the Ninetieth Division through the European campaign.[3] Wherever the division went, so did the Fifty-Ninth. On one occasion the hospital was ordered to pull up stakes and move twice in one day because the front was moving so fast as the Allies advanced deeper into Germany.

This photograph appeared in the Pan American edition of *Yank* magazine on May 18, 1945, and in the victory edition the same month. It shows Second Lieutenant Coeyman from Emmaus, Pennsylvania, ministering to a wounded soldier somewhere in Germany. The war was over, but there were thousands of troops recovering from their wounds.

Coeyman trained as a nurse before the war, joined the army shortly after the war began, and was shipped to England with a large group of nurses. Their vessel arrived on D-Day as thousands of ships were heading to the invasion beaches in France. "We couldn't get off! The harbors were too crowded," Coeyman recalled. After disembarking, her unit spent three weeks preparing to land on the Continent, and the nurses were put to work sewing cloth medical record bags that were placed at the foot each soldier's bed. The bags went with the patient wherever he was sent.

The Fifty-Ninth landed in France in early July and set up tents that served as patient wards and operating rooms. Coeyman administered medications while teams of other nurses assisted the surgeon in the operating room. The

Evangeline
Coeyman during
World War II.

Evangeline
Coeyman, 2014.

unit traveled all the way across France, weathered the Battle of the Bulge, and then followed the front into Germany.

Coeyman returned to the States in December 1945 and went back into nursing. She obtained a BS degree from the University of Pennsylvania and a master's in education from Temple University. She spent her entire medical career at St. Luke's Hospital in Bethlehem, Pennsylvania, retiring in the late 1980s. Today she lives in nearby Allentown and is a member of various World War II veterans groups, including the Veterans of the Battle of the Bulge and the World War Two Roundtable in Allentown.

Kilroy

Kilroy appeared all over the world during World War II, and his image lingered long after the conflict ended. U.S. servicemen doodled the inscription "Kilroy was here" all over the globe during the war. The *New York Times* in 1946 reported that James J. Kilroy was the originator of the phrase.[4] Author Charles Panati says: "The mischievous face and the phrase became a national joke. . . . The outrageousness of the graffiti was not so much what it said, but where it turned up."

James Kilroy, an American shipyard inspector, worked at the Bethlehem Steel Shipyard in Quincy, Massachusetts, and during World War II he used his name to mark the rivets he checked. Workmen were paid by the number of rivets they installed, and riveters would make a chalk mark at the end of their shift to show where they had left off and the next riveter was to begin. Some riveters discovered that if they started work before the inspector arrived, they could receive extra pay by erasing the previous worker's chalk mark and making their own farther back on the same seam, giving themselves credit for some of the previous riveter's work. Kilroy stopped this practice by writing "Kilroy was here" at the site of each chalk mark. At the time, ships were being sent off to war before they had been completely painted, so when sealed areas were opened for maintenance, soldiers would find Kilroy's name scrawled on a bulkhead. Thousands of servicemen may have seen or heard of his slogan on the outgoing ships, and Kilroy's name produced the legend. Afterward, servicemen began placing the slogan on

different places and especially in newly captured areas.[5] While the origin of the slogan is somewhat obscure, that of the cartoon character with the bulbous nose resting on a wall is less so. It is said to have originated with "Chad" in Great Britain before the war, a creation of the cartoonist George Edward Chatterton. Presumably, "Chad" and Kilroy merged during the 1940s with the vast influx of Americans into Britain. The Chad cartoon was very popular in Britain with the slogan "What, no . . . ?" or "Wot, no . . . ?" underneath, as a satirical comment on shortages and rationing. (One sighting, on the side of a British First Airborne Division glider in Operation Market Garden, had the plaintive complaint "Wot, no engines?") The phrase lived in Britain into the 1950s and 1960s and was used in advertising. For instance, in many areas of the country, outdoor toilets were the norm, so a poster advertising indoor plumbing might say, "Wot, no inside lav?"[6]

Kilroy is still known and used today by U.S. servicemen. The phrase was reportedly seen scribbled on barriers on main supply routes (MSRs) and warehouses in Iraq.

Dinner in the Snow

The army photographer who took this image, Arthur H. Herz, was a German immigrant who did not recall how he came to meet Pvt. Thomas O'Brien, his subject in this photo.[7] Blanket draped over his shoulders, O'Brien, of Middleboro, Massachusetts, huddles in the snow-covered Ardennes to eat dinner during the Battle of the Bulge. A foot soldier in the 101st Infantry Regiment, Twenty-Sixth Infantry Division (in peacetime the Massachusetts National Guard division), O'Brien, nicknamed "Red," for his hair, took part in Gen. George S. Patton's Third Army drive to relieve the 101st Airborne Division in Bastogne in December.

"The grim picture — a cold shivering infantryman in the desolate Ar-

Pvt. Thomas O'Brien during the Battle of the Bulge.

Thomas O'Brien in class A uniform.

dennes snow—brought back vividly the most desperate period of my army service," Herz recalled years later. "In addition to fighting the still formidable Wehrmacht in the woods in those January days, we were also facing an icy environment in bitterly cold weather, and we were ill-prepared for it. I vividly recall my futile attempts to requisition an extra army-issue sweater, but none was available until I took one off a killed GI. To some degree the picture seems to capture not only that harsh war situation, but also the determined self-reliance of our soldiers and their heroic fortitude."[8]

Because he was a German immigrant and spoke with a noticeable accent, Herz was arrested by MPs shortly after the Battle of the Bulge began. The Germans had parachuted a number of English-speaking troops behind American lines to disrupt Allied communications, and U.S. troops were wary of spies and infiltrators. Herz spent a week in confinement until he was released on word from his commander. It was a few days later that he took the photo of O'Brien. Herz was wounded a short time later but was luckier than O'Brien. Herz survived the war and had the satisfaction of living into old age and enjoying a sixty-five-year marriage and four children, as well as grandchildren and great-grandchildren. He died in 2012 at age ninety-one. O'Brien was killed in action in January 1945. His family elected to have him buried with comrades in Europe, and he is interred at the Henri-Chapelle American Cemetery in Belgium.

Long Life for Youthful Lookout

This boyish sailor, Lawrence Britton from Arkansas, was nineteen when a navy photographer took his picture while Britton was on lookout duty on the escort carrier USS *Nassau,* ferrying troops and fighter planes to the Aleu-

below left Lawrence Britton during World War II.

below right Lawrence Britton in later life.

The Britton family, 2009.

tians, the island chain that stretches from Alaska into the far North Pacific Ocean.[9] The Japanese invaded the islands of Attu and Kiska in 1942 in what was the only part of North America occupied by the enemy during World War II. The *Nassau* was part of a task force of ships and carried a squadron of planes that provided air cover for ground forces retaking Attu and Kiska.

Later in his stint in the navy, an injury forced Britton's departure from the *Nassau,* but after recuperating he was assigned to the crew of a minesweeper, USS *Scout,* which saw extensive duty in the Philippines and was in Manila Bay when Gen. Douglas MacArthur made his famous return to Corregidor. Britton watched the spectacle through binoculars.

Lawrence Britton joined the navy in 1943 and served until 1946, when he came home and enrolled in the University of Central Arkansas to obtain a degree in accounting. He worked as an accountant until he was eighty and then retired. Britton remarried after his first wife died, and he now presides over a large family. "It was a good life after the war," he said.

Chapter 7

Dorie Miller, Hero at Pearl Harbor

He was arguably the first decorated hero of World War II, and he was a black man.[1] Doris "Dorie" Miller, portrayed by Cuba Gooding Jr. in the film *Pearl Harbor,* manned a machine gun on the deck of the USS *West Virginia* as she sank, and opened fire on attacking Japanese planes, claiming one kill. Dawn on December 7, 1941, found Miller belowdecks on the "Wee Vee," which was anchored in the middle of Pearl Harbor's "Battleship Row," moored alongside the battleship *Tennessee.* As the Japanese planes swept in and torpedoes struck the *West Virginia,* Miller made his way to his battle station in the antiaircraft battery magazine amidships, only to find it destroyed by a bomb blast. He returned topside to help carry wounded men to a makeshift aid station on the main deck before being ordered to the bridge to assist the mortally wounded captain. Unable to help the skipper and enraged at the Japanese planes still bombing and strafing the ship, Miller rushed to a nearby .50 caliber machine gun and began firing back.

Miller had never trained on the gun but later recalled, "It wasn't hard. I just pulled the trigger and she worked fine. I had watched the others with these guns. I guess I fired her for about fifteen minutes. I think I got one of those Jap planes. They were diving pretty close to us."

The *West Virginia,* ripped by bombs and torpedoes, settled into the mud of Pearl Harbor, taking 130 men with her. She would be refloated and sent to Bremerton, Washington, where she was repaired and substantially modernized. She went back into action in 1944 and participated in the invasions of the Philippines, Iwo Jima, and Okinawa. Doris Miller would not go with her.

For his exploits at Pearl Harbor, Miller received the nation's second-highest award for valor, the Navy Cross, presented by Admiral Chester Nimitz, commander of the entire Pacific Fleet. "This marks the first time in this conflict that such high tribute has been made in the Pacific Fleet to a member of his race and I'm sure that the future will see others similarly honored for brave acts," Nimitz said as he presented the medal aboard the aircraft carrier *Enterprise.*[2]

In the spring of 1943 Miller was assigned to the escort carrier *Liscome Bay.* In November the baby flattop joined the fleet for the invasion of the

Gilbert Islands in the Central Pacific. *Liscome Bay*'s aircraft participated in air attacks against the islands of Tarawa and Makin in the Gilbert archipelago and supported Marines attacking the two objectives. On November 23, as the crew prepared to launch planes, a Japanese submarine near Butaritari Island attacked the *Liscome Bay*. A single torpedo struck the ship near the stern, directly under an ammunition magazine, and the ensuing blast virtually ripped the vessel apart. Within minutes the *Liscome Bay* listed and sank. Only 272 of her 860-man crew were pulled from the sea. Miller was among the dead.[3]

Miller was born in 1919, in Waco, Texas, and was a star fullback on his high school football team. He worked in farming before joining the navy in 1939. At the time the only jobs open to black sailors were either in the engine room or as a mess attendant working in the kitchens. Twenty-year-old Doris Miller chose the mess. The military had been segregated since the Revolution, and blacks were relegated to low-prestige assignments and were excluded from serving with whites in combat positions.

Miller was assigned to the *West Virginia* in the Pacific fleet in January 1940. He went to work in the galley and joined the ship's boxing program, eventually winning the Wee Vee's heavyweight title.

On June 30, 1973, the United States Navy commissioned the USS *Miller*, a Knox-class frigate, in honor of Doris Miller.

Maynard "Snuffy" Smith Rises to the Occasion

Maynard H. "Snuffy" Smith Jr. was an improbable hero.[4] Born to a life of affluence in the small town of Caro, Michigan, in 1911, and the son of a successful attorney, Smith developed a reputation early for being an irresponsible troublemaker. His family sent him to a military academy, but it made little difference. After graduating, Smith worked briefly for the Treasury Department and later for the Michigan State Banking Commission. His father died in 1934, leaving him a comfortable inheritance, and Smith quit work at the age of twenty-three to live with his mother in Michigan during the summer and in Florida in the winter. At age thirty-one in 1942, after a brief, unsuccessful marriage, he was ordered to join the army or face imprisonment

Maynard Smith posing with a B-17 waist gun.

for nonpayment of alimony. He appeared for induction in August 1942—in handcuffs and accompanied by a sheriff.[5]

Smith became an aerial gunner in the Army Air Forces and after additional training was promoted to staff sergeant and assigned to the 423rd Squadron, 306th Bomb Group, in Turleigh, England. Snuffy, as he was nicknamed, became a B-17 ball-turret gunner because of his small size. His first mission, was against enemy submarine pens in Saint-Nazaire, France, and the formation encountered heavy flak as it neared the target. "First you hear a tremendous whoosh," he later recalled, "then bits of shrapnel patter against the sides of the turret, then you see the smoke." With "bombs away," the plane headed home, followed by enemy fighters. When they came into range Smith opened fire with his twin .50s, and the enemy returned fire. "I was watching the tracers from a Jerry fighter come puffing by our tail, when suddenly there was a terrific explosion," he later told reporter Andy Rooney. "Whoomp, just like that. Boy it was a pip!" The enemy bullets ruptured gas tanks and set the plane's midsection ablaze.[6]

Fire in the radio room and another in the tail forced some of the crew to bail out, and the bomber's fate was up to Smith, and he became a hero. He fought the flames with extinguishers, his own urine, and with his hands and a sweater. He gave aid to a wounded gunner and manned the guns himself as the enemy fighters continued their attack. Then he went back to fighting the fires, plunging into the radio room and throwing ammunition boxes through a gaping hole in the fuselage so the shells wouldn't explode. The stricken bomber made it to England with the fires under control, all because of Smith's dogged determination to save the plane.

To Smith his heroics were nothing out of the ordinary. "I wasn't there to get a medal," he said. "Like millions of others, I just wanted to get it over with and get home. It was a miracle that the ship didn't break in two in the air, and I wish I could shake hands personally with the people who built her. They sure did a wonderful job, and we owe our lives to them."[7]

The B-17 reached the English coast and landed at the first available airfield, at Predannack, Cornwall, where the charred and battered Flying Fortress skidded to a halt in two sections. There were more than thirty-five hundred bullet and shrapnel holes in the fuselage and wings. All that would be salvaged from the plane were the engines — and the lives of six men.

The pilot recommended Smith for the Medal of Honor, and *Stars and Stripes* correspondent Andy Rooney was the first to interview Smith after the mission. The published account propelled Smith into instant stardom, and it was a role that he enjoyed. Smith flew four more missions and received the first of two Air Medals. He also missed one mission he should have flown. He returned late to his base and missed a briefing. Another gunner flew the mission, and Smith was sentenced to KP (kitchen duty) for a week, where he was working when Secretary of War Henry L. Stimson came to England to present him with the Medal of Honor.

Stimson stepped forward to place the Medal of Honor around Smith's neck while generals saluted.[8] Radio stations across the United States broadcast the events, and listeners waited for Smith to speak. He stepped to the microphone and said, "Thank you."

As the first enlisted airman ever to receive the Medal of Honor, Smith became legendary, but it didn't change him. He remained the man he always had been, and didn't seem to care what anyone else thought.

At Thurleigh he basked in the attention that followed, eagerly signing autographs "Sgt. Maynard Smith, C.M.H." (Congressional Medal of Honor) and took advantage of his "hero" status to sleep late and get additional privileges. Later, he was grounded and given a desk job. In 1944 the group

Smith receiving
the Medal of Honor.

operations officer noted his lack of "any desire to perform his duties in a manner becoming his rank" and recommended his reduction to the rank of private. Finally, in March 1945, Smith was sent home.

The Michigan town of Caro welcomed Smith with a parade and festivities, and two months later, at Miami Beach, Smith was honorably discharged from the Army Air Forces.

After the war, Smith's second marriage, to a girl he fell in love with in England, fell apart. His business dealings were equally unsuccessful. He died in 1984 at age seventy-three.

Authors Jay Zeamer and Joseph Sarnoski's concluding remarks about Smith might serve as an apt obituary:

> Perhaps . . . Andy Rooney's assessment of Sergeant Smith is the most accurate description of the little man's life—Snuffy Smith was a——up. Before he joined the Army and went to war, it seemed that the little guy couldn't do anything right. Becoming a hero didn't change *Snuffy* Smith, he was still a——up. Somehow, however, despite everything else that was wrong in his life, when six lives hung in the balance and a genuine hero was needed, Maynard Smith found something deep within that finally enabled him to do something right. It would be most unfair to begrudge that man the pleasure of leaving behind something good for his family, his hometown, and his nation to remember him for.[9]

Gen. Douglas
MacArthur's
return to the
Philippines,
1945.

"I Shall Return"

Bright blossoms of Bougainvillea grace the island of Corregidor at the
entrance to Manila Bay in the Philippine Islands. In the distance loom the
rugged mountains of the Bataan Peninsula, where American and Philippine
forces held off the Japanese army for months in the spring of 1942 after the
Japanese invaded the Philippines in December 1941. Bataan became infa-
mous after American and Filipino forces on Bataan surrendered and were
force-marched to prison camps, in what became known as the Bataan Death
March. Remnants of the American forces retreated to Corregidor, a rocky
outcropping, in hopes of rescue by an expeditionary force arriving from the
United States. None came, and the besieged defenders fought on hopelessly.

The U.S. high command, knowing that they could not relieve Corregidor, ordered Gen. Douglas MacArthur, the commanding general in the Philippines, to leave and proceed to Australia, where he would take command of growing U.S. forces in the South Pacific. Always dramatic, MacArthur took his leave from Corregidor in March 1942 from Lorcha Dock, the remains of which are visible to this day. He vowed: "I shall return," and he kept his word. Three years later, on March 7, 1945, MacArthur came back to Corregidor after its recapture by American forces.[10]

"Have your troops hoist the colors to its peak and let no enemy ever again haul it down," he said on his return. He was greeted by the ruins of "Topside," the heart of the island's defensive system with headquarters, barracks, ordnance shops, and a movie theater. The ruins of the barracks remain to this day as a reminder of the past struggles on the island.

After MacArthur's departure from Corregidor in 1942, American forces held out for another two months before being overwhelmed by the Japanese, who invaded the island. All who survived were made prisoners of war, and many did not live to tell of their ordeal.

A former superintendent of the United States Military Academy at West Point, army chief of staff in the 1930s, and a Medal of Honor recipient for his defense of the Philippines in 1942, MacArthur went on to lead U.S. forces through New Guinea and back to the Philippines and accepted the Japanese surrender in September 1945 on the battleship *Missouri*. He oversaw the occupation of Japan following the conflict and in 1950 led United Nations forces in the Korean War, until relieved by President Harry Truman in April 1951 for overstepping his authority as a military commander. He appeared before a joint session of Congress to explain his motives and is remembered for his, again, dramatic and sentimental statement of good-bye, taken from an old army barracks ballad: "Old soldiers never die, they just fade away." MacArthur died in 1964 at age eighty-four.

Tom Lea, War Artist

His vivid paintings brought an added dimension to World War II, a reality not captured in photographs. He portrayed rugged Marines in vivid colors, in green and black facial camouflage against a backdrop of the red fire and

black smoke of a burning invasion beach. He captured an assault landing with a depiction of a wounded Marine, his face a bloody pulp and an arm a mass of torn, bloody flesh. Tom Lea painted a portrait of a Marine on Peleliu, in the Palau island group in the Central Pacific, who had seen too much combat and horror; he stares into space in what was called the two-thousand-yard stare.

Lea was an artist and reporter for *Life* who chronicled World War II in the Pacific with brush and oils. His work appeared in the magazine during the war and in large spreads in *Life's Picture History of World War II*, published after the war. In some of his portraits—including that of the exhausted Marine on Peleliu—there is a likeness to Lea himself, particularly the eyes.

Thomas Lea III, born in 1907, was an accomplished muralist, illustrator, war correspondent, portraitist, novelist, historian, and easel painter during his long life, lived mostly in Texas.[11] Like Bill Mauldin, he attended the Art Institute of Chicago, studying from 1924 to 1926 under the noted muralist John Warner Norton. From 1926 to 1933 Lea worked as a mural painter and commercial artist in Chicago, and in 1927 he married fellow art student Nancy Taylor. He then went to Europe to study the masters in Italy.

In 1940 Lea joined the editorial staff of *Life,* and from 1941 to 1946 he was an accredited war correspondent, traveling over one hundred thousand miles to theaters of war where American forces were involved, including the North Atlantic, on board the carrier *Hornet* in the South Pacific, and in China.

Lea wrote about and illustrated his experience of landing with the first assault wave of the First Marine Division on Peleliu in his book *Peleliu Landing,* in 1945. Many of his war paintings came from that bitter struggle, which was expected to last four days but dragged on for two months in the fall of 1944. American casualties were heavy—1,300 killed and 5,450 wounded—and the battle was considered unnecessary by some, because Peleliu had little strategic value. Lea described the circumstance around his war painting in detail as vivid as his paintings. Of the two-thousand-yard stare he wrote: "Down from Bloody Ridge Too Late. He's Finished—Washed Up—Gone. As we passed sickbay, still in the shell hole, it was crowded with wounded, and somehow hushed in the evening light. I noticed a tattered Marine standing quietly by a corpsman, staring stiffly at nothing. His mind had crumbled in battle, his jaw hung, and his eyes were like two black empty holes in his head. Down by the beach again, we walked silently as we passed the long line of dead Marines under the tarpaulins."

A final project for *Life* after the war, depicting the history of beef cattle in the Americas, took Lea to Mexico, where he became fascinated with black fighting bulls. The artist returned to writing, and his first novel, *The Brave Bulls,* in 1949, was a best seller and was made into a movie starring Mel Ferrer. His *The Wonderful Country,* in 1952, was another best seller and movie, this time featuring Robert Mitchum. He wrote a dozen other books

Tom Lea, years
after the war.

about subjects as diverse as mountaineering in Wyoming, horse training in
sixteenth-century New Spain, and the history of the mammoth King Ranch.
His paintings depict remote and exotic places, from Ecuador to China,
but primarily capture subjects found near his home on the border between
Mexico and Texas.

As a portrait artist Lea took pleasure in capturing likenesses, starting
with friends in El Paso, and when he went to war he took on well-known
subjects like Generals Jimmy Doolittle and Claire Chennault, and Madame

and Generalissimo Chiang Kai-shek. Lea wrote, "I select my subjects, they don't select me."

The first dinner given by Governor and Mrs. George W. Bush in the Texas Governor's Mansion was to honor Tom Lea. The governor read from *Tom Lea: An Oral History,* for friends that included Mrs. John Connally, Lady Bird Johnson, and the Kleberg family of the King Ranch. When accepting the Republican nomination for president of the United States in 2000, George W. Bush quoted Tom Lea about living on the "sunrise side of the mountain," and, after his election, he made it known that a Tom Lea painting would hang in the Oval Office. Tom Lea died in 2001 at the age of ninety-four, following a fall at home. Laura Bush traveled to El Paso for the memorial service, the first trip she made as First Lady of the United States. While in El Paso, she requested the loan of Lea's painting *Rio Grande,* from the El Paso Museum of Art, to hang in the Oval Office.

Lea never sought the approval of a critic or the favor of a museum director, placing the majority of his paintings after World War II in the private collections of his personal friends.

Those friends have generously responded to efforts to preserve Lea's work, establishing repositories at the University of Texas at Austin, the University of Texas at El Paso, and the El Paso Museum of Art. Friends have also created the Tom Lea Institute, a not-for-profit corporation, to perpetuate his legacy through collaboration and education.

Chapter 8

Patton's Infamous Slap

This is the man who almost ended Gen. George S. Patton's military career. Pvt. Charles Herman Kuhl was the American soldier who was slapped and kicked by General Patton in an August 1943 incident in Sicily a month after Allied forces landed on the island to begin the conquest of Italy.[1] Kuhl was a soldier in the First Infantry Division who had been making regular visits to a field hospital from the front lines. Doctors diagnosed his condition as "exhaustion" and wrote on a medical chart: "psychoneurosis anxiety state, moderately severe (soldier has been twice before in hospital within ten days. He can't take it at the front, evidently. He is repeatedly returned)."

General Patton, then commander of the U.S. Seventh Army, was visiting the Fifteenth Evacuation Hospital tent when he approached Kuhl's bed, read his chart, and saw that Kuhl had no visible injuries or wounds. Patton asked Kuhl what was wrong, and Kuhl replied, "I guess I can't take it," which sent Patton into a rage. Patton slapped Kuhl with his gloves, grabbed him by the collar, and dragged him to the tent entrance and kicked him, demanding that the officer in charge send the "gutless coward" back into battle.

Kuhl, twenty-six, from Mishawaka, Indiana, wrote his father a few days later: "General Patton slapped my face yesterday and kicked me in the pants and cussed me." He warned his father, "Just forget about it in your letters." The elder Kuhl told the *Daily Journal-World* in Lawrence, Kansas, that his son had been ordered to North Africa for a hearing on the issue and was taken to Patton's office, where the general apologized, shook hands with him, and said he had "acted too hastily."[2]

Charles Kuhl.

The Kuhl incident was the first slapping of an American soldier by Patton. A week later, at the Ninety-Third Evacuation Hospital, Patton found a shivering soldier. Seeing that the young man had no wounds, Patton asked what was the matter. "It's my nerves," replied Pvt. Paul G. Bennett of South Carolina.

"Your nerves hell. You're just a goddamned coward you yellow son of a bitch," Patton shouted. He slapped Bennett and yelled, "Shut up that goddamned crying. I won't have these brave men here who have been shot seeing a yellow bastard sitting here crying." Patton struck Bennett so hard his helmet liner flew off, and screamed at him, "You're going back to the front lines, and you may get shot and killed, but you're going to fight. If you don't, I'll stand you up against a wall and have a firing squad kill you on purpose. In fact, I ought to shoot you myself, you goddamned whimpering coward." Patton pulled out his pistol and threatened Bennett, prompting the chief medical officer to step between the two men.[3]

Bennett reportedly had begged not to be evacuated to a field hospital but was ordered to be admitted by a rear-echelon medical officer. At the evac hospital, Bennett was found to have a fever and exhibited symptoms of dehydration, including fatigue, confusion, and listlessness. His request to return to his unit was turned down by medical officers.

The slapping incidents were covered up for a time but eventually made the news, and Patton was nearly relieved from active duty. He lost command of the Seventh Army, was required to apologize in person to his troops, and was placed in limbo until after the invasion of France on June 6, 1944. In July he assumed command of the Third Army in France and went on to achieve even greater fame as a battle commander.

Following the incident, Kuhl's condition was finally diagnosed; he was suffering from chronic dysentery and malaria. Kuhl later said, "Patton didn't know that I was as sick as I was" and called him "a great general," adding "I think at the time it happened, he was pretty well worn out himself."

Kuhl served for eight months with the First Division. Previously he had been a carpet layer in South Bend, Indiana. After the war he worked as a sweeper for the Bendix Corporation. He died of a heart attack in 1971 at the age of fifty-six. He is buried in Mishawaka, Indiana, where he was born.

A young Gerald Ford going up for a jump ball during a pickup basketball game in the aircraft elevator on the USS *Monterey*,

Future President Plays Hoops

Gerald R. Ford was probably the most athletic of all this nation's presidents. He was a football standout at the University of Michigan, where he played center and linebacker for the Wolverines' undefeated 1932 and 1933 national champion teams. In 1935 he was a member of the collegiate all-star football team that played the Chicago Bears. Hoping to be admitted to the Yale

Sergeant Drabik.

of twenty-eight American soldiers, but by that time other bridges had been hastily built by Army engineers. According to supreme Allied commander Gen. Dwight D. Eisenhower, taking the bridge at Remagen likely shortened the war in Europe by six months.

Born in 1910, Drabik was the son of Polish immigrants who raised thirteen children on a farm near Toledo, Ohio. Prior to his enlistment, he was a butcher in nearby Holland, Ohio. Early in his military career, he distinguished himself by rescuing 120 recruits who were lost in the California desert. Drabik was seriously wounded during the Battle of the Bulge. On August 18, 1945, Toledo honored him and his commanding officer, Maj. Gen. John W. Leonard, with a parade.

Ironically, the man who dodged German bullets on the Remagen bridge died in an auto accident in 1993, en route to a reunion of his unit. He was eighty-two years old.

Hans-Georg Henke — May 1945

This boy's face is the face of Nazi Germany toward the end of World War II in Europe. His name was Hans-Georg Henke, and he was a sixteen-year-old antiaircraft gunner who had joined the Luftwaffe, the German air force, in 1944 after both his parents died. He later said that he was captured on May 1, 1945, six days before the war's end. He is capless, his blond hair disheveled, his air force greatcoat too large, and tears streak his face.[10]

In the final months of World War II in Europe, the Germans recruited

thousands of boys ranging in age from twelve to seventeen to fill the depleted ranks of their dwindling armies. Henke was lucky. Many of these soldiers died in the futile and last-ditch effort to reverse the course of the war in Europe. Some were fanatical Nazis; others, like Henke, were terrified by the experience of war.

Henke was unaware that he was being photographed—presumably, he said, by a Russian or Polish combat photographer who came upon him with a group of fleeing refugees. Why was he crying?

"The retreating German army was blowing up everything as it moved west. The Russians were attacking from the east. Everything around me was chaos. I thought it was the end of the world."[11]

A flak gunner initially sent to Magdeburg to man searchlights against night bombers, Henke served with old men, boys like himself, and even young girls. "We were bombed out, and the dead lay all over," Henke remembered. He was transferred to Berlin, witnessing even greater destruction, and then to Stettin on the Russian front, where his unit was equipped with 88mm guns. The Russians began their final attacks, and Henke and his unit fled west, with the Soviets no more than a kilometer behind them. On May 1 he found himself sleeping in a barn with five remaining members of his unit. Suddenly they heard machine gun fire as the Russians approached, and they all fled for their lives.

We reached an area where refugees, soldiers, and everybody were thrown together. Everything around us was being destroyed. I grovelled in the dirt to find refuge. Sometime while we were there the picture was taken.

The other four left [from his unit] were all men, including the battery commander, a first lieutenant. He asked, "Well boys, what do you want? There are the Russians. Or should we try to reach the Americans? They are 200 kilometers (120 miles) away."

We all voted to try and reach the Americans. We walked eight nights covering about 100 kilometers. We were all wounded. I had a grenade splinter in the foot. I had no shoes, just rags. Everybody had whiskey in their canteens to try and build a little nerve. Then on the ninth day we risked walking in the daylight.

Right away the Russians spotted us. "Hitler kaput," they said. "Go home."

Hans-Georg Henke
in 1967.

We turned back to Berlin and walked another two days. Then we were
captured. The Russians gave the younger ones of us bread and bacon.[12]

Henke was held in captivity until the fall of 1945 and was then released
to go home to Finsterwalde, a small industrial city of thirty thousand, some
sixty miles south of Berlin in what became East Germany. He turned seventeen when he finally reached home. He had two brothers who survived
the war and also returned.

Henke remained in Finsterwalde and joined the Communist Party in
1945. He later married, had a daughter, and lived comfortably in postwar
East Germany until his death in 1997 at sixty-nine.

"For me, when the war ended I was reborn. I was sick of everything that
had happened."[13]

He Spotted Nazi Saboteurs

Seaman John Cullen was a "sand pounder," the term that during World War II the Coast Guard gave its men patrolling the beaches and coastlines of the United States looking for signs of lurking enemy submarines or saboteurs. And in the late spring of 1942, Cullen came upon four German saboteurs recently landed by submarine on a darkened beach near Amagansett on eastern Long Island.[14]

It was on a Saturday, June 13, just six months after the United States declared war, when Cullen spotted a figure in the mist and the shapes of three others. It was "so foggy that I couldn't see my shoes and once in a while you might run into somebody, but very rare," Cullen remembered. Armed only with a flare gun for sending signals, he shined his flashlight at the group, calling out "Who are you?" His Coast Guard insignia was visible. The man closest to him said that he and his companions were fishermen who had run aground. He spoke English well enough, but one of the others, dragging a bag, shouted something in German.[15]

The leader of the group then dropped all pretence, asking Cullen if he had a mother and father who would presumably grieve for him. The man did not display a weapon but said, "I wouldn't want to have to kill you."[16]

The German saboteur, later identified as Georg Dasch, then offered Cullen $300 in cash, saying, "Why don't you forget the whole thing?" Seeing a chance to escape, Cullen took the money and promised he would never identify the men. (He later found he was shortchanged; he had been given $260.)[17]

Cullen fled back to his station and led fellow Coast Guardsmen to the spot of the encounter, where they found no one but dug up buried explosives.

So began a hunt for saboteurs who had been sent to the United States on U-boats by the Germans in a plot to blow up rail facilities and war-industry plants. There were eight men involved—the four who landed on Long Island and another four who arrived in Florida.

The four Amagansett enemy agents took the Long Island Railroad into Manhattan, where they hid for a week. Then Georg Dasch, shaken by his encounter with Cullen, surrendered to the FBI, hoping he would be regarded

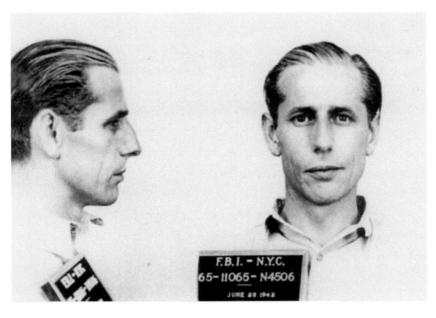

Georg Johann Dasch, Nazi saboteur.

as a hero in America by exposing the plot. His fellow conspirators were rounded up.

Seaman Cullen was about to become a hero. He was awarded the Legion of Merit and was much ballyhooed, appearing at news conferences, participating in parades, ship launchings, and war bond drives. He remained stationed in the States during the war, serving as the driver for high-ranking Coast Guard officers.

John Cornelius Cullen was born in 1920 in Manhattan but grew up in Queens, New York. He enlisted in the Coast Guard a few weeks after the Japanese attack on Pearl Harbor. After the war he worked as a dairy company sales representative on Long Island and lived in nearby Westbury. He died in 2011, at age ninety, in Chesapeake, Virginia, where he had retired with his wife, Alice, in the early 1990s.

Cullen was described as "a thoroughly wholesome, typically American boy" with "a modest demeanor." He played down the hero angle when he appeared at a Coast Guard news conference in 1942. "The German fellow was nervous," he said, "but I think I was more nervous."[18]

Georg Johann Dasch, the saboteur, was born in Speyer, Germany. He entered a Roman Catholic seminary at the age of thirteen to study for the priesthood but was expelled the following year. Lying about his age, he enlisted in the German army and served in Belgium during the final months of World War I. In 1923 he entered the United States illegally by ship as a stowaway and enlisted as a private in the Army Air Corps, serving for one year, and was honorably discharged. He worked as a waiter in New York City and in 1930 married Rose Marie Guille, an American citizen. Naturalized an American citizen in 1933, Dasch returned to Germany in 1941.

At a secret military trial in Washington, Cullen identified Dasch as the man he had encountered on the beach. Six of the eight saboteurs, four of whom came ashore in Florida, were executed on August 8, 1942. President Roosevelt commuted the life sentence for Dasch and a second saboteur, Ernst Peter Burger. In 1949 Dasch and Burger were released from prison and deported to Germany, but they were not welcomed, being regarded as traitors who had caused the death of their comrades. Dasch died in 1992 at the age of eighty-nine at Ludwigshafen.

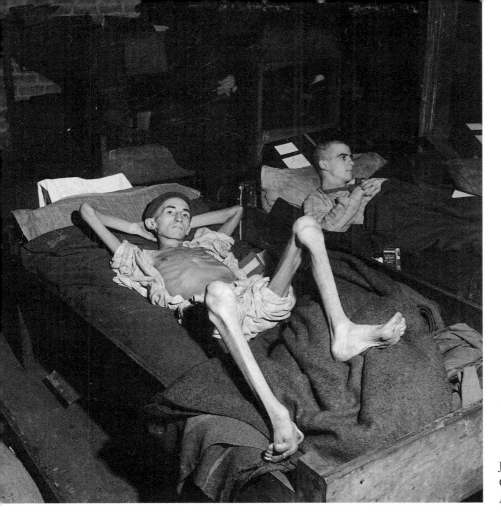

Joseph Demler in a German prison camp, April 1945.

Joseph Demler, Human Skeleton

Being a prisoner of war in Nazi Germany, particularly in the last year of the war, often meant starvation. The Germans barely had enough food to feed themselves. Bernard V. O'Hare, Kurt Vonnegut's fellow POW, mentioned in Vonnegut's novel *Slaughterhouse-Five*, spoke of always being hungry and continuously thinking and dreaming of food.[19]

When American forces reached Pvt. Joseph Demler in Stalag 2-A in Limburg, Germany, on March 29, 1945, he was near death, suffering from malnutrition, dysentery, pneumonia, and pleurisy. Because army medics and doctors didn't have a scale that registered low enough, they estimated that Demler weighed between seventy and seventy-five pounds and said he was within three days of dying. The POW next to Demler in the prison camp infirmary died a few hours after this photograph was taken, as did many other of his fellow POWs as medics tried to save them. Few could take food, and they threw up what they did eat, because their shrunken stomachs rejected solid nourishment.

A *Life* magazine photographer visiting the POW camp that day took Demler's photograph while he lay in bed, too weak to move. The photo appeared on the cover of *Life,* April 16, 1945, under the caption "Human Skeleton."

Demler's odyssey as a prisoner of war began a few days after the start of the Battle of the Bulge on December 16, 1944. Demler had joined the army in June 1944 and was shipped overseas as an infantry replacement, landing in Marseille, France. Along with hundreds of other newly arrived troops, he was trucked to Nîmes and then assigned to the Thirty-Fifth Infantry Division in Belgium that was attached to Gen. George S. Patton's Third Army. When the Germans launched their Ardennes offensive in December—the Battle of the Bulge—Demler's company went into action, but his stint as an infantryman lasted just four days. He remembers being in a farmhouse when a German tank fired a round that blew out the first floor. He survived, but his company was surrounded, and most of the men were taken prisoner. The Germans stripped the Americans of all possessions and began marching them east toward a POW camp near Limburg, about sixty miles southeast of Cologne. The prisoners were first forced to work repairing railroad tracks destroyed by Allied bombing, and they had to be watchful for American P-61 Black Widow night fighter bombers that ranged across Germany, shooting up anything that moved and bombing the railroads. The men slept in warehouses without blankets and were then loaded onto railroad freight cars, where for four days without relief they were packed so tightly that they had to stand. They went without food and water, and the latrine was a lard bucket at one end of the car. The man next to Demler died, as did several other men during the ordeal.[20]

Demler and his comrades arrived at their POW camp in February, and soon he was stricken with a variety of ailments, including dysentery, beriberi—a vitamin B1 deficiency—and eventually pneumonia. His medical problems were exacerbated by a lack of food. Nevertheless, he never lost hope. "I never got a defeated attitude," he said. "You had to think positively." Hope was maintained by the influx of newly arriving American POWs, who brought word of the Allied advance into Germany. Liberation couldn't be that far off. When the American army finally arrived, Demler was immediately given heavy doses of penicillin and sent to a field hospital, where he was operated on the next day. Doctors took out part of a rib, inserted a tube, and drained out four liters of pus. "The Lord was with me," Demler said with a laugh. He was then shipped to the Forty-Eighth General Hospital in Paris, where his strength and weight were built up. He was flown back to the States as a litter case and sent to Kennedy General Hospital in Tennessee as a patient along with six thousand other wounded and sick servicemen. He went home to Port Washington, Wisconsin, on November 29, 1945. He then weighed 120 pounds.

At first, Demler suffered from occasional nightmares from his ordeal, but he settled down, went to work, and raised a family of two boys and a daughter.[21]

Joseph Demler, 2013.

Ten years later, Demler appeared in *Life* again; the magazine went to Port Washington to do a follow-up article.[22] Then, weighing 155 pounds, he was thriving, although he wore a brace to support a weak back and shoulders, and he had problems with his teeth. *Life* did a multi-photograph spread of Demler in his new life, showing him bowling, tending to his lawn and garden, clerking at the post office, where he hoped to obtain a permanent position, and eating a hearty meal cooked by his wife, Therese, whom he married in 1951. The article appeared on April 4, 1955, under the headline "pow's Recovery." He became a letter carrier and assistant postmaster of Port Washington, a small city of just over eleven thousand, some twenty-five miles north of Milwaukee.

Despite his ordeal as a pow, Demler is active today, still in Port Washington at age eighty-nine and attending veterans' events, particularly the Honor Flights that take elderly veterans to Washington, D.C., to visit the World War II Memorial. From his experience as a human skeleton, Demler took away several important lessons. He learned to pray and that every day is a bonus.

Chapter 9

Sudden Death in Poland—1939

On September 1, 1939, Nazi Germany marched into Poland in an invasion that marked the beginning of World War II. The Poles were helpless against the onslaught and capitulated a few weeks later. The Germans had begun to practice their new form of warfare, called *Blitzkrieg*—lightning war. On the ground, tanks swarmed over the battlefield to overwhelm the enemy's ground forces, and in the air, waves of German warplanes laid waste to cities. Warsaw was badly bombed before the Poles surrendered, and the city's residents were cut off from everyday supplies.

On September 13, a group of women and young girls were foraging for potatoes in a field near Warsaw when a flight of two German bombers suddenly appeared over them. The foragers flattened themselves on the ground as the Germans opened fire with machine guns and dropped bombs that landed wide and struck a nearby house. The women in the field escaped injury, but two people in the house were killed. The women continued their search for food, but the German planes reappeared, sweeping in low with their guns blazing. A young girl was caught in the fire and killed, along with another woman.[1]

This photograph depicts ten-year-old Kazimiera Mika mourning the death of the young girl, her older sister, killed in a field near Jana Ostroroga Street in Warsaw. The photographer, Julien Bryan, was filming the war when Kazimiera returned from hiding to find that her sister had been killed in the attack.

Bryan described the scene:

> As we drove by a small field at the edge of town we were just a few minutes too late to witness a tragic event, the most incredible of all. Seven women had been digging potatoes in a field. There was no flour in their district, and they were desperate for food. . . . Two of the seven women were killed [in the German attack]. The other five escaped somehow.
>
> While I was photographing the bodies, a little ten-year-old girl came running up and stood transfixed by one of the dead. The woman was her older sister. The child had never before seen death and couldn't understand why her sister would not speak to her. . . .

Kazimiera Mika, Warsaw, Poland, 1939.

end. In the photo series Lott was featured in a wheelchair on the magazine's cover, January 29, 1945.[4]

Life assigned photographer Ralph Morse to the story. "I was with the Third Army in France when a cable arrived from my editors in New York," Morse told Life.com.

> They wanted me to cover a guy, they said, who was wounded bad enough
> that he had to go all the way home. . . . I showed the cable to [Gen. George
> S.] Patton. I had just done a cover story on him for Life, so I was friendly
> with him. I said, "General, look at this. They're never even going to let
> me get in an ambulance with a wounded man! They'll need that spot for
> another wounded guy."
>
> Patton reads the cable and says, "Look, you tell the editors at Life to get
> in touch with the surgeon general of the United States Army, and get a set
> of orders with your name on them as a wounded man who has to get all
> the way back to the States. Get that, and send it to me." So Life went to
> Washington . . . and got the order.

With orders in hand, Morse hung out in the aid station waiting for a seriously wounded soldier to appear. "I was with Lott's division in mid-November," Morse remembered:

> I showed one of the doctors my orders and he told me they'd look for a
> likely candidate. We're pinned down by German mortar rounds, and they
> bring in a wounded soldier. The doctor looks at this young man's wound and
> tells me, "This will only take him as far as London." But I need someone
> who's going to be sent all the way home. The mortars let up a little and I
> head out with some of the medics, who went out to try and bring back some
> of the wounded. The mortars start pouring in again and we start running
> back to the barn that's serving as a base and a hospital, and I hear Lott
> say, "Oh! I've been hit in both arms." We got him back to the aid station,
> and he's lying on the hay on the floor of the barn and the doc looks at him
> and then looks at me and says, "He's your man." And that's how the story
> started.[5]

It was the beginning of a forty-five-hundred-mile journey by ambulance, train, and plane through Paris, London, and finally to a hospital in Michigan.

Morse shadowed Lott through two more field dressing stations and five hospitals, making a photographic record not only of countless operations to restore his shattered arms but the painful rehab he endured on his way home. *Life* noted that 96 percent of the wounded that reached hospitals survived their wounds.

At an evacuation hospital in Nancy, surgeons took X-rays that revealed that the bones in both arms were shattered and that muscle and blood vessels had been torn away. They could do little more than clean the wounds and immobilize him in a plaster cast. One surgeon wrote on his record, "watch circulation in his right hand carefully: amputation of the arm will probably be indicated." The photograph above shows Lott in great pain as he gets a new cast at a hospital in England. He was given a sedative but was kept conscious to ensure that the cast was a good fit. Gas gangrene infections had attacked his wounds, delaying his evacuation to the States.[6]

Lott's next stop was at Rhoads General Hospital in Utica, New York, closer to his home in upstate New York. He was regaining feeling in his hand, and doctors were hopeful that he would regain the use of both arms once they repaired the damage to the bones. Because of the article, Lott received thousands of letters while recuperating, his arms immobilized in improvised casts. Many letters were from young girls, but many were from mothers who had sons in the military and whose sons had been wounded or killed.[7]

Lott was born in Endicott, New York, was orphaned at the age of two, and grew up in foster homes in various New York state communities. He ran away from a foster home at age fifteen, then joined the army in 1943 and was in action in France in the fall of 1944 when wounded. He called several upstate New York cities home but said he had no next of kin and no circle of friends. His hope upon release from the hospital was to "settle down as an independent and able-bodied man with a job."

In 1947 Lott remained hospitalized, and *Life* sent Ralph Morse to Percy Jones General Hospital in Battle Creek, Michigan, for a follow-up article and photo series. There were still forty-two thousand GIs in U.S. hospitals recuperating from war wounds. Lott had had five operations and twenty-five hundred injections of penicillin, but his right arm remained severely deformed. Doctors later determined that amputation of the arm was best because it was so badly damaged and had become useless. It would be another year, 1948, before Lott was released from the army and from the hospital.[8]

George Lott was something of an enigma. After returning to the United States and after the 1947 *Life* article, he disappeared from view. Then, in 1961, the *Albany (N.Y.) Knickerbocker News* printed an article about him in which Lott reflected on his ordeal sixteen years earlier in France. He said the mortar explosion that wounded him blew him into a creek. When he tried to use his arms, his hands were useless. A fellow soldier helped him walk back to an aid station. After two years of convalescence he asked doctors to amputate his right arm because it "was so much dead weight. If I placed a cigarette in my right hand and forgot about it, it would burn me. I wouldn't feel it, but I could smell the burning flesh."

In 1961 Lott lived in a second-floor apartment in Albany with his dog, Beatrice. When he felt like fishing, he went fishing. The same with hunting. And occasionally he stayed out late to have a few beers. Lott lived "an easy going life"; he had had enough excitement during the war to last a lifetime.

Lott had a full disability pension from the Veterans Administration and eventually moved to 9 Pine Street in Albany. He told neighbors that he had no immediate or extended family. Lott became something of a quiet recluse and didn't speak much about his war experience. "He was the kind of guy who would sit on his front porch and drink a beer," said one acquaintance. "He was friendly but would respond with a 'yes' or a 'no' to questions. He was a very private man." George Lott died in March 1995 at age seventy-five, with no will and no family but with a substantial estate, estimated to be valued at about $600,000, which was administered by the courts. Apparently Lott did have some family after all. A lengthy search turned up a few nieces and nephews. George Lott is buried in Albany.

Ralph Morse outlived Lott by many years. He died in 2014 at age ninety-seven.

Through Death Valley

This photograph depicting Pfc. Paul Ison in a running crouch as he dodges Japanese machine gun fire on Okinawa in May 1945 has become iconic and something of a symbol of the Marine Corps and intrepid Marine infantry. It shows Ison as he raced through an area nicknamed "Death Valley" by the Marines, to assist in the demolition of an enemy bunker. On the day the photograph was taken the Marines sustained 125 casualties crossing Death Valley, so named because it was continuously swept by enemy machine guns.

The Americans invaded Okinawa in early April 1945, and the struggle to take the island from the Japanese lasted eighty-two days. The Marine Corps Historical Center lists American losses in the battle as 7,374 killed, 31,807 wounded, and 239 missing in action. The navy reported 34 U.S. ships sunk, 368 damaged, 763 aircraft lost to all causes, 4,907 seamen killed or missing in action, and 4,824 wounded. Beyond the magnitude of these losses by the Americans, an estimated 110,000 Japanese soldiers were killed in the battle for Okinawa, more than in any previous Pacific battle.[9]

Ison made three runs through Death Valley that day. The first was in the morning. The second was to return to an ammunition dump to pick up the explosives just behind the lines, and the third run was to return with the explosives to the demolition site. The photo was taken when Ison was twenty-eight and an assistant BAR (Browning Automatic Rifle) gunner.

Ison appears to be wearing a BAR cartridge belt but is also carrying an M-1 rifle. He has an entrenching shovel as well, and also has M-1 bandoleers around his neck and is wearing leggings. The First Marine Division had a standing order that its troops would wear leggings during the battle. The Sixth Marine Division wore them under their trousers. With his cartridge belt and the rest of the gear, Ison was likely assisting a BAR man.

In an interview in 1984 that appeared in *Leatherneck Magazine*,[10] Ison recounted his career in the Marine Corps and the events that day, May 10. He went to an ammunition dump to get satchel charges and was told they had already been moved to the front. He dashed forward through the draw between two ridges of "Death Valley" and was told by his captain that the charges had not been sent forward and were still back at the dump. Ison raced back, collected ninety-six pounds of TNT, which he and comrades then carried back. It was on one of these runs that a photographer took his picture. "I got ready to go first and saw photographer (Pvt Bob Bailey) aiming a camera at me. I didn't slow down to wave or smile, believe me!"[11]

Ison tried several times during the early part of the war to enlist but was turned down because he was married with four children. He went to work in a factory making engines for B-17s and B-29s but was always aware that people would look at this strapping young man and wonder why he was not at war. "I was gung ho and loved my country," Ison said. As the war dragged on, restrictions were eased, and at twenty-eight, he became a Marine. He shipped out of San Diego to the Russell Islands. He thought he would wind up with a desk job in New Guinea but was originally chosen to be the man who carries a flamethrower. He was assigned to the First Marine Division that landed on Okinawa and was engaged in combat until the end of the campaign, and then was shipped to China for occupation duty. He returned home after the war and eventually settled in Fort Myers, Florida. He died in October 2001.

Okinawa was a prelude to invasion of the Japanese home islands, and the ferocity of the battle and the casualties incurred gave American military planners pause. The Americans also knew that the Japanese were preparing for an invasion and were assembling thousands of Kamikazes to attack American targets. Thousands of Japanese soldiers would have met the U.S. invasion and even thousands of Japanese civilians, many training to kill with nothing more than wooden spears. Estimates of the number of American casualties to subdue the Japanese homeland were in the hundreds of thousands to over a million men dead, wounded, and missing. The dropping of the atomic bombs in August 1945, though considered controversial by some, saved many thousands of American lives.

Patsy Caliendo: The Long Journey Home

There was no family in attendance, no old friends or neighbors, no family plot, just a few GIs and a chaplain saying a few words of prayer on a bleak, muddy landscape of recently dug graves and deep pits for the expected arrival of more newly dead American soldiers. This was the manner in which hundreds of thousands of Americans, killed in World War II, went to their final rest, wrapped in a mattress cover. The cemetery above, Henri-Chapelle in Belgium, was ever-expanding the final months of World War II as more and more soldiers were killed in the final push into Nazi Germany.

The GI being buried among the thousands of crosses at Henri-Chapelle in March 1945 was Patsy Caliendo, a twenty-nine-year-old army private from 264 North Sixth Street, Brooklyn, New York. Caliendo was killed in action near Kerpen, Germany, while serving with C Company, Twelfth Engineer Combat Battalion, Eighth Infantry Division. He was first listed as missing in action and later declared killed in action. Born in 1916, Caliendo entered

Pvt. Patsy Caliendo is buried at the Henri-Chapelle American Cemetery, 1945.

the U.S. Army on March 25, 1941.[12] He attended schools in Brooklyn and was a machinist in civilian life.

During World War II none of the soldiers killed were immediately returned to the United States for burial. The supplies of war to and from the States took precedence, and the bodies of the fallen were interred near where they fell. The Henri-Chapelle Cemetery was established as one of several European burial ground for the thousands of young men killed. After the war Henri-Chapelle became a permanent American Cemetery for World War II soldiers, harboring the remains of more than eight thousand GIs killed in Europe. Today it is a beautiful memorial to America's World War II dead and not the busy, unkempt burial ground it was in 1945 with yawning, pre-dug graves awaiting the next remains. In wartime, the bodies of the dead were unceremoniously stacked in the beds of two-and-a-half-ton trucks near where they were killed and transported to various nearby cemeteries. The remains were then placed in standard-issue mattress covers, and a chaplain was present with the burial squad.

Caliendo's burial at Henri-Chapelle was only the beginning of his long journey home to New York. Following the war, families of those killed were asked if they wished to return their dead to America or leave them buried among their comrades overseas. The Caliendo family, his mother Palmina and his father Angelo, along with 233,000 other American families, asked that their son be returned. In 1947 Patsy Caliendo was disinterred from his grave at Henri-Chapelle, his remains were autopsied and placed in a steel coffin. Army physicians who reviewed Caliendo's body found that bullets or shell fragments had shattered his arms and legs. Next, Caliendo's coffin, along with 6,248 others carrying the remains of war dead, was loaded aboard the USAT (U.S. Army Transport) *Joseph V. Connolly,* a Liberty Ship specially converted to carry hundreds of coffins back to the United States. This was the first shipment of remains transported home from Europe to the United States, and it arrived in New York harbor on October 26, 1947. Thus began one of the most solemn processions in New York's history.

The *Connolly* arrived in New York harbor in an early morning haze accompanied by two navy destroyers and a gleaming white Coast Guard cutter whose crews stood at attention. On the *Connolly*'s boat deck an honor guard surrounded a solitary, flag-draped coffin that stood out in the diffuse morning light, a swath of red, white, and blue against the ship's gray flanks. The casket, bearing an unknown Medal of Honor recipient killed in the Battle of the Bulge, was a symbol of all the young men who were coming home on the *Connolly* and of the thousands of other war dead who were to follow in the months and years ahead. The operation to return America's World War II dead did not end until 1951, but to this day, remains of the dead from that war are unearthed every year and returned for burial in the United States.

As the *Connolly* approached Manhattan's towering skyline, the battleship *Missouri,* anchored in the Hudson River and recently back from Tokyo Bay, where the Japanese surrender had taken place on its deck, boomed a salute with her sixteen-inch guns that echoed through the city's man-made canyons. A flight of fighter planes roared overhead before gracefully turning away, leaving the city in an unnatural quiet. A lone Marine on one of the destroyers sounded Church Call.

The *Connolly* slipped into Pier 61 at Manhattan's West Twenty-First Street, and the heavy steel sarcophagus was removed from the deck and carried ashore by pallbearers representing all the nation's armed services and placed on a caisson that was hitched to an armored car. A bugle sounded, onlookers wiped away tears, and the procession began, solemnly, quietly, six thousand men strong, as it moved up Fifth Avenue, past the ranks of four hundred thousand New Yorkers who lined the sidewalks on this warm autumn day to pay final tribute to the nation's war dead.

This was a very different procession from the one two years earlier in 1945 when frenzied, elated, and war-weary New Yorkers welcomed the return of their proud and triumphant fighting men who marched along the same route in battle dress. The war had been won, and all thoughts were to the future and to the living, not to the past and to the dead. General Dwight "Ike" Eisenhower was the star of the parade, standing in the back of an open limousine, arms outstretched and giving his broad smile. The din from the cheering crowds filled the avenue, and a festive blizzard of ticker tape and confetti swirled down to blanket the street along the way. The parade route was festooned with signs: "Welcome Home" and "Well Done." The people of New York were delirious.

In October 1947, the old welcome signs from '45 were still visible, but faded, and an eerie silence greeted the ranks of soldiers as they marched up Fifth Avenue, stopping briefly in Madison Square. They moved on, through the shadow of the Empire State Building on Thirty-Fourth Street, past the library on Forty-Second Street, and on to Central Park. There were no roaring crowds, no confetti or ticker tape, only the sound of muffled footsteps and the hollow clop of horses' hooves. Many in the crowd sobbed openly and prayed as the military formations passed with the caisson following behind.

The marchers turned into Central Park at Seventy-Second Street and advanced into the Sheep Meadow, where forty thousand mourners had assembled to see the casket carried to a purple-and-black catafalque. As the day wore on and a heat haze settled over the Sheep Meadow, the crowd swelled to 150,000. Chaplains of three faiths offered prayers for the souls of the war dead, and then officials from city, state, and federal government spoke. At 4 p.m. a seven-man honor guard fired a three-volley salute, a drummer began a slow roll, and a mournful taps sounded across the park as

Grave of Patsy
Caliendo in Queens,
New York City.

the setting sun backlit the skyline to cast ever-lengthening shadows across
the Sheep Meadow. Another distant bugler beyond a stand of trees echoed
with faint, quivering notes. The pallbearers returned the casket to the caisson
as the West Point Band played "Nearer, My God, to Thee." The casket was
carried away and returned to the *Connolly*, whence the bodies of the 6,248
war dead would be returned home by train to large cities and small towns,
where they would be greeted by an honor guard of veterans and then reburied
in a family plot or in a national cemetery.[13]

For Patsy Caliendo, the trip to his local cemetery was hardly two miles
away from where the *Connolly* was docked. He was buried in the Caliendo
family plot in St. John Cemetery, Queens, in November 1947. He was home.
Today he rests beside Palmina and Angelo, his mother and father.

Chapter 10

Retrieving *Chow-hound*

Chow-hound had served with the Eighth Air Force for four months when this photo was taken on March 8, 1944, on a Ninety-First Bomb Group strike against the Erkner ball-bearing works near Berlin. The B-17 had already seen its share of combat flying and had sustained damage from enemy antiaircraft. On its fifteenth mission, a flak splinter tore a hole in the nose art, right in the stomach of the cartoon dog, Chow-hound, who was drawn lazily draped over a falling bomb. Ground-crewmen repaired the plane and painted a purple heart next to the dog, indicating that it had suffered wounds. *Chow-hound* continued to fly missions over Europe well into the summer of 1944 from its base at Bassingbourn, England. Heavy bombers were often diverted from missions over Germany to attack targets in France to aid Allied ground forces struggling to break out of Normandy after the D-Day invasion. *Chow-hound* may well have participated in Operation Cobra, when hundreds of heavy and light bombers, along with fighter planes from England, dropped twenty-five hundred tons of bombs on German front-line positions in Normandy in late July. Cobra broke the German grip on the Normandy bridgehead and enabled American forces to break through enemy lines and begin a rapid advance across France.

If *Chow-hound*'s luck held out, it would become an old, worn-out B-17 assigned to the graveyard for spare parts. The bomber's good fortune, however, lasted only until August 8, 1944, when it was again on a mission over France and was hit by flak. The ensuing explosion was powerful enough to tear the plane apart, and it crashed to earth, the tail section falling one way and the fuselage spinning another to land in a farm field. None of the crew survived.[1]

End of story? No! Fifty-eight years later, in 2002, a French group hunting World War II aircraft crashes explored *Chow-hound*'s site just south of the town of Lonlay-l'Abbaye and found debris from the B-17. They contacted the American Joint POW/MIA Accounting Command, which searches for the eighty-eight thousand military personnel who remain unaccounted for from World War II. American personnel were sent to France in June 2004 to bring what remained of the plane home to the United States, along with any human remains they found.[2]

On the day *Chow-hound* went down, villagers buried four of the dead crew members, while the bodies of two others were later recovered by advancing American ground troops. But three of the crew remained unaccounted for: Tech. Sgt. Henry F. Kortebein of Maspeth, New York, 2nd Lt. David J. Nelson of Chicago, and Tech. Sgt. Blake A. Treece Jr. of Marshall, Arkansas. A nearby farmer had collected the debris of *Chow-hound* that rained down on his fields and dumped it in the largest crater left from the crash. He filled the hole and topped it with fresh soil, and cows grazed over it for six decades.[3]

The crash site was still used for farming when the American search team arrived in 2004. "Lot of cows, lot of cheese," said a team member. "Quiet little quaint Normandy farming communities." "The search took a month, using backhoes, rakes, and buckets. The team found parts of the airplane itself, including two engines, parts of the wings, and the hind legs of the dog painted on the nose." *Chow-hound*'s identification was confirmed by the serial number recovered from a .50 caliber machine gun.[4]

The team also found six 250-pound bombs. "It got dangerous for us to continue," said one participant. An explosive ordnance professional was called in to disarm the bombs and safely cart them away.

The remains of the three missing crew members were discovered in the wreckage. Those of Sergeant Kortebein of Maspeth consisted of bones from his right shoulder and right forearm. There was enough for mitochondrial DNA testing, a technique often used in identifying such remains, and the bones were sent to the Joint POW/MIA Accounting Command laboratory in Hawaii. As the identities of the missing crewmen were known, the command contacted Sergeant Kortebein's sister in Arizona for a blood sample and got a match. The command turned the remains over to the family. Relatives of the three crewmen were allowed time with the caskets when they were returned to the United States on a C-17 cargo plane.

The story of *Chow-hound* came to an end sixty-two years after her last mission over France in 1944, when the last three crewmen were buried on August 25, 2006. The plane is remembered also by its likeness in a Revell ¼8 scale model.

Three Who Might Have Become Supreme Commander instead of Ike

In early 1943, Operation Torch, the campaign to defeat the Germans and Italians in North Africa, was not going well for three-star general Dwight D. Eisenhower, the commander of British and American forces in the theater. The inexperienced Americans were no match for the battle-wise and hardened Germans led by Field Marshal Erwin Rommel. In February 1943 Rommel attacked American First Division troops in the Kasserine Pass, soundly defeating them and driving a fifty-mile wedge in Allied lines. As overall commander, Eisenhower had to take responsibility for the crushing defeat and was concerned that his reputation had been sufficiently tarnished as a commander that he would be relegated to an insignificant command after the campaign ended.

Gen. Frank Andrews.

Army Chief of Staff Gen. George C. Marshall had earlier sent "Ike" in 1942 to England to begin organizing for the hundreds of thousands of American troops who would be transported to the British Isles in preparation for the coming invasion of continental Europe. Eisenhower was later picked to lead the invasion of North Africa in the fall of 1942, and he gave up his position as European commander in England.

In his place as European commander, General Marshall chose Lt. Gen. Frank Maxwell Andrews, a highly respected Marshall protégé who was one of the founders of the Army Air Corps and a proponent of heavy bombers, particularly the B-17. The grandson of the Confederate cavalry officer Gen. Nathan Bedford Forrest, Andrews was appointed to his new post in January 1943. His tenure, however, was short-lived. In early May he set out on an inspection tour and was killed in the crash of his B-24 bomber as it attempted to land at an air base in Iceland. In his memoirs, Gen. Henry "Hap" Arnold, commander of American Air Forces during World War II, asserted that if Andrews had lived he would have been appointed as supreme commander in Europe and led Allied forces on D-Day. Andrews Air Force Base outside Washington, D.C., is named for General Andrews.[5]

Following Andrews's death, Marshall appointed another protégé as European commander, Lt. Gen. Jacob Devers—"Jakie" to his friends—who had been chief of the army's armored forces. Devers assumed the European command and began planning the cross-channel invasion. Devers had risen rapidly as war approached and is credited with expanding the nation's armored forces and developing the Sherman tank, the standard American tank used during the war. As European commander he was in a position to lead the D-Day invasion as supreme commander but ran into resistance from Prime Minister Winston Churchill, who preferred dealing with the more diplomatic Eisenhower than the blunt-spoken Devers. With the North African campaign ending in victory for the Allies, Eisenhower replaced Devers, who was sent to North Africa to lead American forces in the Mediterranean and to plan the invasion of southern France in August 1944.[6] The story is not complete without mention of Gen. Joseph W. Stilwell, known to his men as "Vinegar Joe," because of his caustic personality. He was also called "Uncle Joe" by his troops because of his concern for the ordinary GI. Stilwell was considered one of the top corps commanders at the outset of World War

Gen. Jacob Devers.

Gen. Joseph W. Stilwell.

II and was initially selected to plan and lead the invasion of North Africa, the assignment Eisenhower would later have. But Marshall and President Roosevelt changed course and assigned Stilwell as the top U.S. general in the China-Burma theater, with the objective of keeping China in the war fighting the Japanese. Early in his career Stilwell had spent three tours of duty in China and was the American military attaché in Beijing from 1935 to 1939. He spoke Mandarin fluently and knew the Chinese leaders and the ins and outs of China's politics. Marshall and Roosevelt called on Stilwell, against his objections, to return to China, where he had often tangled with Chiang Kai-shek. Had Stillwell been the general in charge of the North African invasion and been successful, he well might have been appointed as supreme commander in Europe.[7]

It was Eisenhower who became supreme commander, a hero and future president. The world knows him as "Ike." If the others had been given the command we would likely have had a war hero and maybe a president nick-named "Jakie," "Vinegar Joe," or just plain "Frank."

Tony Hillerman, Future Mystery Writer

Tony Hillerman was a decorated hero of World War II who became one of the premier mystery writers of the latter half of the twentieth century.[8] In his depiction of life and crime on the Navajo reservation in the Southwest, he shed light on Native American culture and brought it to life for readers through Navajo tribal police officers Sgt. Jim Chee and Lt. Joe Leaphorn, who dealt with mayhem and mystery through many of Hillerman's novels.

Hillerman began writing mysteries, as well as novels and memoirs, in the 1960s after a career in journalism. He gained intimate knowledge of the Navajo, Hopi, and Zuni tribes while growing up and living around them. "It always troubled me that the American people are so ignorant of these rich Indian cultures," he once said. "I think it's important to show that aspects of ancient Indian ways are still very much alive and are highly germane even to our ways." Hillerman served in the army as a mortar gunner in World War II and saw action in France, the Low Countries, and Germany. He was a

Future writer
Tony Hillerman
decorated for
bravery.

member of a company that started out with 212 men but was whittled down
to only eight who remained of the original complement.[9]

In a patrol behind enemy lines in Germany in 1945, he stepped on a mine
that shattered his leg, foot, and ankle and left him with facial burns and
temporary blindness. He also lost partial sight in his left eye. For his wartime
service Hillman was awarded the Silver Star, the Bronze Star with oak leaf
cluster, and the Purple Heart.

Hillerman was born in Sacred Heart, Oklahoma, in 1925 and attended
a boarding school for Native American girls, where he was one of only a

Hillerman, center,
seated, with army
buddies.

Tony Hillerman
later in life.

few farm boys enrolled. The school was near a Benedictine mission to the Potowatomie tribe, where he absorbed much Indian lore. He graduated from Konawa High School in 1942 and returned to farming after a brief sojourn in college and after his father's death.

After the war, he received a bachelor's degree from the University of Oklahoma and continued his travels through the Southwest, where he mingled with Native Americans. He then worked as a journalist, political reporter, and editor for a variety of newspapers in the Southwest before becoming UPI bureau manager in Santa Fe and later working as editor for the *Santa Fe New Mexican.* He joined the journalism faculty of the University of New Mexico in 1966 and began writing, turning out eighteen mystery novels in his Navaho Series set in the Four Corners area of New Mexico, Arizona, Colorado, and Utah. Lieutenant Leaphorn was introduced in Hillerman's first novel, *The Blessing Way,* in 1970, the second book in the series. *Dance Hall of the Dead* won a 1974 Edgar Award from the Mystery Writers of America for best novel.

Hillerman told PBS in 1996, "I am seventy-one, have now-and-then rheumatic arthritis but now very badly, have in-remission cancer, have had a minor heart attack, have one mediocre eye, one tricky ankle and two unreliable knees due to being blown up in World War II."

His memoirs were published in October 2001. They won the Agatha Award for best nonfiction. Hillerman, who resided in Albuquerque, New Mexico, died in 2006 at age eighty-three.

The Man Who Dropped the Bomb

Stephen Ambrose, the historian, once called Col. (later brigadier general) Paul W. Tibbets "the best flyer in the Army Air Force." Tibbets, however, is best remembered as the pilot of the B-29 *Enola Gay,* which dropped the atomic bomb dubbed "Little Boy" on the Japanese city of Hiroshima on August 6, 1945. The mission, along with a second atomic bombing, of Nagasaki a few days later, effectively ended World War II. The Japanese, many of whom would have fought on to the death, surrendered on August 14.[10]

Tibbets had been a B-17 pilot in the European theater and was the lead

Col. Paul Tibbets, 1945.

pilot on the first American bombing raid over Europe in August 1942. Two months later he led the first flight of one hundred b-17s against industrial targets in Lille, France. When Lt. Gen. Dwight Eisenhower needed a lift from England to North Africa prior to the invasion of North Africa, Tibbets was selected to fly the future supreme commander and president.[11]

When the United States began testing its new bomber, the b-29, the chief of the Army Air Forces, Gen. "Hap" Arnold, called on Tibbets to lead in the development of the "Superfortress" that later carried out a prolonged bombing campaign against Japan. A year later he was tapped to lead the 509th Composite Group of fifteen b-29s and eighteen hundred men designated to train for the eventual dropping of the atomic bomb.[12] The group was assigned to the island of Tinian in the Marianas, which had been wrested from the Japanese in 1944. On August 6, 1945, with Tibbets at the controls,

the *Enola Gay,* named for his mother, took off just before dawn for the two-thousand-mile flight to Hiroshima. The bomb detonated at 8:15 a.m. on a cloudless, hot day and left a towering mushroom cloud that rose thousands of feet in the air. The bombing led to the deaths of an estimated ninety thousand Japanese.[13]

Tibbets received the Distinguished Service Cross for the mission. He remained in the air force after the war in various commands and retired in 1966 as a brigadier general. He went into business and retired in 1987. He died in 2007 at the age of ninety-two. During his lifetime Tibbets was portrayed numerous times; Barry Nelson played him in *The Beginning of the End,* in 1947, and Robert Taylor played him in *Above and Beyond,* in 1952.

The *Enola Gay* lives on. The B-29 was carefully restored and now is on exhibit at the Smithsonian Steven F. Udvar-Hazy Center in Chantilly, Virginia.

The *Enola Gay,* seen on Tinian island during World War II. The plane has been restored and is displayed at the Smithsonian's Steven F. Udvar-Hazy Center in Chantilly, Virginia.

The Saga of *Lady Be Good*

In 1958 prospectors searching for oil deposits deep in the Libyan desert came upon a strange sight: the well-preserved wreckage of a World War II B-24 bomber. The plane appeared to have made a near-perfect landing in the barren wasteland several hundred miles from the Mediterranean coast. The fuselage was broken in two, the nose was shattered, and debris lay scattered about, but the plane appeared remarkably intact for crash landing and was preserved as though it had only recently been forced down. The prospectors notified U.S. Air Force personnel, and investigators converged on the site to find water bottles in the plane, oil still in the engines, and the radio and machine guns in working order. But where was the crew? There was no evidence that they had landed with the plane.[14]

Investigators went to work and found that the plane, named after the popular 1920s song "Lady, Be Good," had disappeared after a mission in April 1943 from her base in Benghazi, Libya, to Naples, Italy. Search planes were dispatched in the hours after her disappearance, but no trace was found, and after the war further searches were conducted for *Lady Be Good* and other missing aircraft. It was assumed that the plane went down in the Mediterranean with the loss of her entire crew.

In 1958 teams searched nearby for the crew but found nothing. But investigators knew *Lady Be Good*'s flight path on its return from Naples to Benghazi and, speculating that it overflew the base, began to search backward from the wreckage toward Benghazi. Their calculations proved correct. Deep in the desert, miles from where the plane came down, they found evidence of the crew — empty shell casings, signal flares, and other debris. They believed the casings were from shots fired by the pilot to rally any crew members who had landed nearby after bailing out.

If the pilot and copilot had parachuted with the crew, why didn't the plane crash headlong into the desert? The only answer investigators could surmise was that *Lady Be Good* kept on flying until it ran out of gas and then glided along until it pancaked on the desert floor. One engine was discovered to have been operating when the plane hit the ground.

Investigators now had a point of reference, and by intuition, careful plot-

The B-24 *Lady Be Good* in the Libyan desert, 1960.

ting, and sporadic finding of artifacts, they began to locate the bodies of the men—only bones seventeen years after the plane came down. In all they found the entire crew, but one. In reconstructing events it was found that the men had set out for the coast not knowing how hopeless were their efforts. One by one the bodies were found in separate locations, the last closer to safety than the others, but still miles away.

One interpretation of why *Lady Be Good* was lost was that her navigator misinterpreted radio signals from the Benghazi base. The plane had taken off with a flight of B-24s to bomb Naples but had aborted the mission and turned back toward Benghazi following a radio signal emanating from the airfield. But the signal went both ways and could be picked up north or south of the base. There was no way of distinguishing whether a plane was over the Mediterranean heading toward the base or out over the Sahara heading away. The crew may have believed the plane was over the Mediterranean when they bailed out.

A diary kept by copilot Robert Toner during the group's trek to reach safety recorded the haunting struggle of the men to survive and their belief that they were near the coast when in fact they were many miles distant. The men had but one canteen of water as they trudged north, leaving behind a trail of boots, scraps of parachutes, Mae West vests, and markers for would-be rescuers. The group survived for eight days in the brutal heat and frigid nights and traveled eighty miles from the crash site. A group of three continued another twenty and twenty-seven miles farther as the others waited for help, too exhausted to keep moving.

The remains of the crew were given formal burials back home, but the plane still lay in the desert. Later the Libyan government retrieved most of the wreckage, which was last located at a Libyan air base. A propeller from *Lady Be Good* is on display at the Museum of the United States Air Force in Dayton, Ohio. The saga of *Lady Be Good* is over, except for the lone crewman who was never found. His remains to this day are somewhere in the vast Libyan desert.[15]

Lone Survivor at Midway

On June 4, 1942, Ensign George H. Gay Jr., a naval aviator, took off from the aircraft carrier *Hornet* with Torpedo Squadron Eight to attack the Japanese fleet approaching Midway Island, northwest of the Hawaiian Islands. The Japanese objective was to capture the island base from the Americans and gain control of much of the North Pacific. Gay and his fellow aviators were flying obsolete Devastator torpedo bombers and stood little chance of surviving the mission. Once the enemy fleet was found, the Americans prepared to attack but immediately were attacked by a swarm of Japanese Zero fighter planes. The air battle was short-lived, and every American plane was shot down. Gay was the last to go down, and he crashed his plane into the sea in the midst of the enemy fleet, which consisted of four aircraft carriers and accompanying cruisers and destroyers. Gay hid under a seat cushion from his plane to protect against being strafed by Zeros and awaited rescue. He never would have imagined that he had been given a ringside seat to a spectacular Japanese defeat and the turning point in the Pacific war.

As Gay's squadron was being wiped out, other American carrier planes were winging their way toward the Japanese fleet. To prepare for the oncom-

Torpedo Squadron Eight prior to the Battle of Midway, June 1942. Ensign Gay is center, bottom row.

Ensign
George H. Gay.

ing Americans, the Japanese had recovered their fighter planes to rearm and refuel them, which they were still doing when the American planes arrived overhead. The Americans attacked immediately, catching the Japanese planes on the carrier decks. Within minutes the four Japanese carriers were aflame, all were sunk, and the Americans had won what could be described as the most decisive battle of World War II in the Pacific. While three years of bitter fighting lay ahead, the Japanese navy never was able to replace the carriers lost at Midway, while the Americans produced scores of flattops, whose planes pounded Japanese forces from the South Pacific to Japan.

Gay watched the disaster unfold as he bobbed about in the water "cheering and hollering with every [American] hit." He was rescued the next day by a seaplane searching for survivors. He received the Navy Cross, and Torpedo Squadron Eight received the Presidential Unit Citation. Recovered from wounds sustained during the battle, Gay served in the Guadalcanal campaign. A hero after his ordeal and featured on the cover of *Life* magazine, he made numerous public appearances in support of the war effort. After the war he remained in the naval reserve and was a pilot for Trans World Airlines (TWA) for thirty years. He died in 1994 at age seventy-seven.[16]

Bomb Blast on the *Enterprise*

This unique photo depicts the moment a Japanese bomb exploded on the flight deck of the U.S. aircraft carrier *Enterprise* during action in the Battle of the Eastern Solomons in the South Pacific in August 1942. *Enterprise* was operating with Task Force Sixty-One to support U.S. Marine landings on Guadalcanal and Tulagi in the Solomon chain and was guarding seaborne lines of communication southwest of the Solomons. The battle began on August 24 when a strong Japanese naval force was spotted two hundred miles north of Guadalcanal. The Americans attacked with carrier-based aircraft and sank the Japanese light carrier *Ryujo*, but Japanese planes inflicted heavy damage on the *Enterprise*, with one of the enemy bombs landing on the flight deck as seen in the image above. Quick work by the crew limited the damage, and the *Enterprise* made it back to Hawaii on her own steam for repairs.

The caption provided by the military for this photograph states that the explosion killed Photographer's Mate 3rd Class Robert F. Read. It would seem likely, since Read was very close to the blast. However, the naval historian Samuel Elliot Morison, in his *History of U.S. Naval Operations in World War II,* states that Read was killed by a bomb that had earlier hit the after starboard five-inch/38-caliber gun gallery, which can be seen burning in the upper left. Morison further states that the bomb seen here exploded with a low-order detonation, inflicting only minor damage. But minor damage to the superstructure of an aircraft carrier would be major damage to the human body. So who took the photo, and did he survive? From the proximity of the blast it would seem—probably not.[17]

Notes

CHAPTER 1

1. Albro T. Gaul, "We March in Paris," *American Philatelist,* November 1, 1988, 1032–48.

2. Cecil B. Currey, *Follow Me and Die* (Briarcliff Manor, NY: Stein and Day, 1984).

3. Following identifications in this section from Gaul, "We March in Paris."

4. Gaul, "We March in Paris."

5. Ibid.

6. National Archives and Records Administration (NARA), "The War in the Pacific," "Joseph Timothy O'Callahan and the U.S.S. Franklin," www.archives.gov.

7. Joseph Timothy O'Callahan, *I Was Chaplain on the Franklin* (New York: Macmillan, 1956).

8. "O'Callahan Society," Alumni.holycross.edu.

9. Robert Blanchard, interview with David P. Colley, October 8, 2006.

10. The account of Moore and his family is based on Stephen Buttry, "An American Story, the Life and Times of a Midlands Family," *Omaha World Herald,* November 9, 1997.

11. Ibid.

12. Ibid.

13. The following account of Jackson's life is based on "Graham Washington Jackson, Navy Musician," obituary, *New York Times,* January 20, 1983.

14. Ibid.

CHAPTER 2

1. The following account of Holmes is based on Ann Palmer (daughter) interview with David P. Colley, June 14, 2008.

2. The following account of the life of Milford Abijha Sellars is based on Daniel Sellars (son) interview with David P. Colley, March 15, 2007.

3. Account based on Louise Bratton (widow) interview with David P. Colley, September 12, 2005.

4. Account based on Julio "Julie" Bescos interview with David P. Colley, January 23, 2006.

5. Bratton interview.

6. Ibid.

7. Ibid.

8. Bescos interview.

9. Ibid.

10. Peter Maslowski, *Armed with Cameras: The American Military Photographers of World War II* (New York: Free Press, 2008), 272.

11. Ibid.

12. Ibid.

13. Lee Weiser (brother-in-law), interview with David P. Colley, October 29, 2012.

CHAPTER 3

1. Joel Kurth, "The Man with Ike Dies at 77," *Saginaw (MI) News,* August 29, 1999, 1.

2. Ibid.

3. Tracy Calabrese, "Saginaw's Famous 'Unknown Soldier' Brushes Off Notoriety," *Saginaw (MI) News,* June 6, 1989.

4. "Teacher Recalls D-Day for Class," www.508pir.org.

5. The following account based on James Barron, "The Model for 'Rosie,' but What Is a Rivet?," *New York Times,* May 19, 2002, 37.

6. Ibid.

7. C. L. Sulzberger, *The American Heritage Picture History of World War II* (New York: American Heritage, 1966), 432.

8. Account drawn from David P. Colley, *Safely Rest: A Father's Quest to Discover the Fate of His WWII Soldier Son* (New York: Berkley Caliber, 2004).

9. Quoted ibid.

10. The following account based on Faris Tuohy interview with David P. Colley, July 6, 2006.

11. Letter from Faris Tuohy to David P. Colley, December 2014.

CHAPTER 4

1. The following account based on Wayne Terwilliger e-mail exchange with David P. Colley, January 10, 2007.

2. Ira Berkow, "At 80, a Manager Keeps Going and Going and . . . ," *New York Times,* December 7, 2005.

3. Terwilliger, e-mail exchange.

4. Ibid.

5. Ibid.

6. Berkow, "At 80, a Manager Keeps Going."

7. The following account based on Kenneth Averill interview with David P. Colley, October 15, 2005.

8. Sarah Parke, "Famous Pilot's Widow Visits *Memphis Belle* and the Museum of the US Air Force," www.nationalmuseum.af.mil, February 2, 2006.

9. "*Wee Willie* and the Photo That Started It All," www.ww2research.com.

10. The following account based on "*Rose of York,* a Fortress Fit for a Princess," www.vintagewings.ca.

CHAPTER 5

1. Bill Mauldin, *The Brass Ring, A Sort of Memoir* (New York: W. W. Norton, 1972).

2. Ibid.

3. The following account based on Cynthia Gordon, "Palmer Man's Path to Postal History Was All in a Day's Work," *Express-Times* (Lehigh Valley, PA), February 19, 1999, 1.

4. See "WWII's B-17 *All American:* Separating Fact and Fiction," http://www.warbirdsnews.com/?s=All+American.

5. Ibid.

6. Ibid.

7. Ibid.

8. See Charles B. MacDonald, *A Time for Trumpets* (New York: William Morrow and Co., 1985), 488–513.

9. See Carroll V. Glines, *The Doolittle Raid: America's Daring First Strike against Japan* (Atglen, PA: Schiffer Publishing, 2000).

CHAPTER 6

1. "F6F-5 Hellcat Fighter of U.S. Navy Pilot Ensign John Fraifogl," http://ww2db.com/image.php?image_id=6330.

2. "John George Fraifogl—Obituary," http://ww2db.com.

3. Evangeline Coeyman, interview with David P. Colley, July 7, 2009.

4. See "Who Is 'Kilroy'?," *New York Times*, January 12, 1947, 30 (magazine).

5. Ibid.

6. Ibid.

7. The following account based on Arthur Herz, Robert Faro, and James Ditano interviews with David P. Colley, 2011.

8. Ibid.

9. The following account based on Lawrence Britton interview with David P. Colley, March 11, 2008.

CHAPTER 7

1. National Geographic.com, "Ship's Cook Third Class Doris 'Dorie' Miller," Beyond the Movie, Pearl Harbor, http://www.nationalgeographic.com/pearlharbor/ngbeyond/people/.

2. Great Black Heroes, Doris Miller, wwwgreatblackheroes.com.

3. Ibid.

4. Following account based on "SSgt. Marynard 'Snuffy' Smith,

Medal of Honor Recipient," Honor Flight Arizona, June 2, 2013, www.honorflightaz.org.

5. Susan Howe, "SSgt Maynard 'Snuffy' Smith," ibid.

6. "Maynard H. Snuffy Smith," www.homeofheroes.com.

7. Howe, "SSgt Maynard 'Snuffy' Smith."

8. "Maynard H. Snuffy Smith," www.homeofheroes.com.

9. See "May Day Massacre," www.homeofheroes.com/wings/part2 /06_smith.html.

10. John Costello, *The Pacific War, 1941–1945* (New York: Harper Perennial, 1981), 213.

11. See Tom Lea Institute (biography), www.tomlea.com.

CHAPTER 8

1. See Peter Dekever, "Patton Pressured into Apology," *South Bend (IN) Tribune,* July 18, 1999, F8.

2. Associated Press, "Private Writes of Patton Incident," in *Lawrence (KS) Daily Journal,* November 23, 1943.

3. Martin Blumenson, *The Patton Papers, 1940–1945* (Boston: Da Capo, 1996), 331–32.

4. Gerald R. Ford, biography, Gerald R. Ford Presidential Library and Museum, Ann Arbor and Grand Rapids, MI.

5. Ibid.

6. The following account based on "Alexander Drabik, 82, First GI to Cross the Remagen Bridge in 1945," obituary, *New York Times,* October 2, 1993, 31.

7. Ibid.

8. Howard J. Langer, ed., *World War II: An Encyclopedia of Quotations* (Westport, CT: Greenwood Press, 1999), Alexander Drabik, 206.

9. *New York Times,* "Alexander Drabik, 82."

10. See "Hans-Georg Henke, 16 Year Old German Soldier Crying," Rarehistoricalphotos.com.

11. "Crying Soldier of 16 Now Is East German Communist," Associated Press story appearing in *Spartanburg (SC) Herald-Journal,* March 26, 1967, A5.

12. Ibid.

13. Ibid.

14. See Dan Rattiner, "70th Anniversary," *Dan's Paper,* danshamptsons. com, April 27, 2012, 15.

15. Richard Goldstein, "John Cullen, Coast Guardsman Who Detected Spies, Dies at 90," *New York Times,* September 2, 2011.

16. Ibid.

17. Ibid.

18. Ibid.

19. Account based on interview with Bernard V. O'Hare (who was captured with Kurt Vonnegut in 1944), by David P. Colley, 1984.

20. Following account based on Joseph Demler interview with David P. Colley, 2014.

21. Ibid.

22. See "PW's Recovery, Joseph Demler Thrives at Home," *Life,* April 4, 1955, 135–36.

CHAPTER 9

1. Julien Bryan, *Warsaw 1939 Seige; 1959 Warsaw Revisited* (Warsaw: Polonia, 1959), 20–21.

2. Ibid.

3. Julien Bryan, "Poland Then and Now," *Look,* September 1, 1959.

4. Ralph Morse, "George Lott, Casualty of War," *Life,* January 29, 1945, 15.

5. Life.Time.com, "Behind The Picture: George Lott, Wounded Warrior."

6. Ibid.

7. Letters, "George Lott, Casualty, Has Received More Than 3,000 Letters," *Life,* February 26, 1945.

8. John Dennis, attorney for the estate of George Lott, 2012.

9. John Costello, *The Pacific War, 1941–1945* (New York: Harper Perennial, 1981), 578.

10. Tom Bartlett, "Death Valley Photo," *Leatherneck Magazine,* April 1985.

11. Ibid.

12. Caption, Associated Press photo and Department of the Army, U.S. Army Human Resources Command, Patsy Caliendo Individual Deceased Personnel File.

13. Colley, *Safely Rest*, 1–6.

CHAPTER 10

1. See Michael Wilson, "After Six Decades, 3 Who Died in French Field Are Home," *New York Times*, August 25, 2006, 25.

2. Ibid.

3. Ibid.

4. Ibid.

5. Lt. Gen. Frank M. Andrews, printable fact sheet, National Museum of the United States Air Force.

6. Russell F. Weigley, *Eisenhower's Lieutenants: The Campaigns of France and Germany, 1944–1945* (Bloomington: Indiana University Press, 1981), 82–83.

7. Barbara W. Tuchman, *Stilwell and the American Experience in China, 1911–45* (New York: Macmillan, 1971), 243.

8. Marilyn Stasio, "Tony Hillerman, Novelist, Dies at 83," *New York Times*, October 27, 2008.

9. Ibid.

10. See Richard Goldstein, "Paul W. Tibbets, Jr., Pilot of *Enola Gay*, Dies at 92," *New York Times*, November 1, 2007.

11. Ibid.

12. Ibid.

13. Ibid.

14. "Desert Gives Up Its Secret: 17-Year Mystery of the *Lady Be Good*," *Life*, March 7, 1960 (cover story).

15. National Museum of the United States Air Force, "Lady Be Good" (printable fact sheet), February 7, 2011.

16. "Oral History—Battle of Midway," Navy Department Library, www.history.Navy.mil.

17. "USS *Enterprise*," www.theussenterprise.com.

Illustration Credits

The author wishes to thank the following sources and all of the individuals, families, museums, and organizations that generously granted permission to use their images.

INTRODUCTION

Page xvi: National Archive and Records Administration (NARA)

CHAPTER 1

Page 2: AP Images/Peter J. Carroll
Page 5: AP Images/Peter J. Carroll
Page 7: National Archive and Records Administration (NARA)
Page 8: Courtesy of College of the Holy Cross
Page 9: National Archive and Records Administration (NARA)
Page 10: Bob Blanchard
Page 11: United States Navy
Page 12: Reprinted with permission from the *Omaha World-Herald/Buddy Bunker*
Page 13: Reprinted with permission from the *Omaha World-Herald/Buddy Bunker*
Page 16: Ed Clark, the LIFE Picture Collection/Getty Images

CHAPTER 2

Page 20: National Archive and Records Administration (NARA)
Page 22: Ann Palmer
Page 24: National Archive and Records Administration (NARA)
Page 27: National Archive and Records Administration (NARA)

Page 28: United States Navy

Page 29: Southern California Golf Association

Page 30: United States Navy

Page 31: National Archive and Records Administration (NARA)

Page 32: Toledo-Lucas County Public Library

CHAPTER 3

Page 34: National Archive and Records Administration (NARA)

Page 38: Angel Franco/The *New York Times*/Redux

Page 40: Franks family

Page 41: Museum of the United States Air Force

Page 43: Franks family

Page 44: Franks family

Page 46: National Archive and Records Administration (NARA)

Page 48: Faris Tuohy

CHAPTER 4

Page 50: National Archive and Records Administration (NARA)

Page 53: National Archive and Records Administration (NARA)

Page 55 (top and bottom): Museum of the United States Air Force

Page 57: National Archive and Records Administration (NARA)

Page 58: Museum of the United States Air Force

Page 60: National Archive and Records Administration (NARA)

CHAPTER 5

Page 62: Copyright by Bill Mauldin (1944) Courtesy of the Bill Mauldin
    Estate LLC

Page 64: National Archive and Records Administration (NARA)

Page 65: United States Postal Service

Page 67: National Archive and Records Administration (NARA)

Page 68 (top): The *Virgin Islands Daily News*

Page 68 (bottom): Museum of the United States Air Force

Page 71: United States Army

Page 73: National Archive and Records Administration (NARA)

Page 74 (top and bottom): Museum of the United States Air Force

CHAPTER 6

Page 76: National Archive and Records Administration (NARA)

Page 79: Evangeline Coeyman

Page 80 (top): Evangeline Coeyman

Page 80 (bottom): David P. Colley

Page 83: United States Army

Page 84: Ditano Family

Page 85 (top): National Archive and Records Administration (NARA)

Page 85 (bottom, left and right): Lawrence Britton

Page 86: Lawrence Britton

CHAPTER 7

Page 88: United States Navy

Page 91: Museum of the United States Air Force

Page 93: Museum of the United States Air Force

Page 94: National Archive and Records Administration (NARA)

Page 96: Copyright James D. Lea, courtesy the Tom Lea Institute, El Paso

Page 98: Copyright James D. Lea, courtesy the Tom Lea Institute, El Paso

CHAPTER 8

Page 102: *South Bend Tribune*

Page 105: National Archive and Records Administration (NARA)

Page 107: National Archive and Records Administration (NARA)

Page 108: National Archive and Records Administration (NARA)

Page 109: John Florea, Keystone/Getty Images

Page 111: AP Images

Page 112: United States Coast Guard

Page 115: John Florea, the LIFE Picture Collection/Getty Images

Page 117: Visual Image Photography

CHAPTER 9

Page 120: Julien Bryan, United States Holocaust Memorial Museum

Page 123: Ralph Morse, the LIFE Picture Collection/Getty Images

Page 127: National Archive and Records Administration (NARA)

Page 130: AP Images/William C. Allen

Page 133: David P. Colley

CHAPTER 10

Page 136: National Archive and Records Administration (NARA)

Page 139: Museum of the United States Air Force

Page 141 (top): York County Heritage Trust

Page 141 (bottom): United States Army

Page 143: Anne Hillerman

Page 144: Anne Hillerman

Page 146: Museum of the United States Air Force

Page 147: Museum of the United States Air Force

Page 148: Museum of the United States Air Force

Page 151: United States Navy

Page 152: United States Navy

Page 153: United States Navy